LANDMARK COLLECTOR'S LIBRARY

THE SPIRIT OF COLWYN BAY: 1

THE 20TH CENTURY IN PHOTOGRAPHS

Eunice Roberts & Helen Morley

Acknowledgements

During the compilation of this book, we have received a lot of assistance from many people for which we are very grateful, amongst these the following helped on a more substantial basis;

Conwy Library, Information and Archives Service: Rona Aldrich, County Librarian and Archivist; Susan Ellis, Senior Archivist; and Patsy Carmichael, Archive Assistant; Malcolm Thomas, Senior Community Librarian and all staff at Colwyn Bay Library
Sally Armitage
Margaret Flint
Ian Gamon
John Roberts, Bay of Colwyn Town Council
E. Emrys Jones
Nancy Jones
Paul & Rhian Jones
Andrew & Debbie Morley
Ray & Ray Morley
Peter & Gladys Rickards
Dewi Roberts
Gareth Roberts
Dave Williams

Bibliography

ANDERSON, V. R. & FOX, G. K.
An Historical Survey of Chester to Holyhead Railway (Oxford Publishing, 1984)

BEARDSWORTH, Monica
Penrhos College 1880-1980, the Second Fifty Years

EDWARDS, Geoffrey
The Borough of Colwyn Bay, a Social History 1934-1974 (Colwyn Borough Council, 1984)

MATTHEWS, Gwenda M.
Colwyn Bay Community Hospital, History and Development 1898-1993
(Hospital League of Friends, 1993)

PRICE, Geoff
A Nostalgic Look at Llandudno and Colwyn Bay Trams since 1945
(Silver Link Publishing, 1997)

ROBERTS, Graham
Colwyn Bay and district, a collection of photographs, Vols. 1-3 (Bridge Books, 1991-1997)

SWAINSON, Mary
The Life & Times of Penrhos College 1880-1995 (Laureve Publishing, 1996)

THOMAS, Dilys
Memories of Old Colwyn (Bridge Books, 2000)

TUCKER, Norman & JONES, Ivor Wynne
Colwyn Bay, its history across the years (Landmark Publishing, 2001)

TURNER, Keith
The Llandudno & Colwyn Bay Electric Railway (Oakwood Press, 1993)

LANDMARK COLLECTOR'S LIBRARY

THE SPIRIT OF
COLWYN BAY:1

THE 20TH CENTURY IN PHOTOGRAPHS

Eunice Roberts & Helen Morley

Landmark Publishing

Published by

Ashbourne Hall, Cokayne Ave
Ashbourne, Derbyshire DE6 1EJ England
Tel: (01335) 347349 Fax: (01335) 347303
e-mail: landmark@clara.net
web site: www.landmarkpublishing.co.uk

1st edition

ISBN 1 84306 050 7

Printed by Bookcraft, Midsomer Norton, Somerset
Design by Ashley Emery
Cover by James Allsopp

Front cover: Men at work close to the junction of Nant-y-Glyn Rd

Back cover top: Main Rd through Old Colwyn c.1905
Middle: Domestic Bazaar. Conwy Rd c.1911
Bottom: Rhos Abbey Hotel. Demolished 2001

Title page: Seaview Rd, looking towards St Paul's Church

Contents

Introduction

The original idea for the book seemed an intriguing challenge, to capture the spirit of a century of life in the Colwyn Bay area, embracing so much change along the years. Gradually it became clear that the amount of material covered the project very well, enough for two books!

The obvious subject matter of street scenes, the pier and prom were relatively easy to put together, but the real fun came when finding the more unusual pictures which unlocked fascinating studies of bygone times long forgotten .... here lies the worth of this book, it records a snapshot of the good, special and difficult times in and around our town, its daily life which at times would seem so uneventful, but which now seems to adopt an element of curiosity about it.

Those occasions, the scale of which will never be repeated, such as the May Queen ceremony, the inclusion of buildings only recently demolished, e.g Rhos Abbey Hotel and Penrhos College, their disappearance altering the landscape forever, but not yet gone from our memory.

This book will reinforce with its readers the stature and importance that Colwyn Bay once had, not only as an elegant and prominent seaside town but as an area one was considered lucky to live in.

May Queen processsion in Colwyn Bay

Colwyn Bay's magnificent Victoria Pier and Pavilion which was officially opened on Saturday, June 2nd, 1900.

Everything you might need for an enjoyable early 20th century visit to the seaside – a stroll along the promenade, a visit to the Pier, a dip in the sea with modesty being preserved by the ample provision of bathing huts at the water's edge and lively entertainment on the promenade. The Pier was initially built at a width of 40 feet and a length of just 316 feet, as shown here, and extended later.

The first pile in connection with the first section of the Pier was driven on June 1st, 1899, the architects and engineers, Messrs. Mangnall and Littlewoods, Manchester, carried out the work. The contractors were the Widnes Foundry Company, the Pavilion being constructed by Messrs. William Brown and Son, Salford.

The construction of the Pier continued with the aid of this winding gear set up on the beach. A steam train can be seen passing in the background. When completed, the Pier would be 1,050 feet in length, terminating in a landing stage and head for open-air performances, with shelters.

The "Pioneer" Souvenir

—or—

The Victoria Pier & Pavilion,

COLWYN BAY,

Opened Saturday, June 2nd, 1900,

—BY—

Madame Adelina Patti

(Baroness Cederstrom).

PRICE THREEPENCE.

M. JULES RIVIERE.

By favour of a Special Sitting given May 30, 1900, to Mr. T. W. Thomas, Photographer, Colwyn Bay, for Publication by the "Welsh Coast Pioneer."

Printed and Published by W. H. EVANS & SONS LD   The "Pioneer" Offices, Colwyn Bay and Chester.

Monsieur Jules Riviere was the musical director of the new Pavilion. Born in Paris on November 6th, 1819, a musician and conductor who had conducted orchestral concerts all over the United Kingdom, he had moved to Llandudno in 1887, and until 1893 worked with the Llandudno Pier Company. He then accepted the invitation to Colwyn Bay, and was responsible for securing the services of the "Queen of Song" Madame Adelina Maria Clorinda Patti, Baroness Cederstrom, for the Pavilion's opening concert on June 2nd, 1900. Monsieur Riviere's advanced years made it necessary for a deputy conductor, Henri Verbrugghen, to be appointed. The Pier Company engaged Aime F. Lalande as Secretary and Manager.

The Pier Pavilion could accommodate 2,500 people. The interior was described as follows: "The floor falls towards the orchestra for purposes of sight, and is divided into first and second-class seats; the better seats being upholstered with velvet pile cushions. The stage is designed for high-class concerts, and at the same time made applicable for theatrical plays, operas. The scenery and drop curtain have been painted by Mr. Hart, of London, a well-known scenic artist. The stage is fully equipped with dressing rooms for artistes, including band, and a room for musical director and manager."

BIJOU THEATRE

PIER HEAD : COLWYN BAY

TWICE DAILY : 3 & 8 : TWICE DAILY

A. McALLISTER'S

(MAC)

SUPREMES

A Concert Party of Distinction

8 Star Artistes 8

Everything of the Best in Song & Dance

M A T I N E E

TODAY : 3-0

MATINEES : Commence 3-0 p.m. Doors Open 2-30
EVENINGS : 8-0 p.m. Doors 7-20 Early Doors 7-0

PRICES OF ADMISSION INC. TAX
Booked Seats 1/10 Other Seats 1/3 & 9d.

McAllister's Follies and Supremes, the Summer Revellers and many other entertainers used to put on their summer shows at the Bijou Theatre, at the Pierhead. Built in 1917, the 600-seat theatre burnt down on July 28th, 1933 – it was never replaced.

This view of the Pier and the original Pavilion also shows the Bijou Theatre at the Pierhead. Destroyed by fire on July 28th, 1933, the North Wales Weekly News reported the raising of the alarm: "The fire was first discovered about 4 a.m. by Mr. Hugh Hughes, signalman, Oxford House, Bay View Road, who was on duty in a box near the station. He shouted the alarm through a megaphone, and succeeded in attracting the attention of the sorting staff at the General Post Office, opposite his box. The sorting staff immediately summoned the Fire Brigade, which arrived on the scene within twelve minutes of the discovery". The theatre was destroyed and the Pierhead was burnt through in several parts. Jack Rowlands' Summer Revellers lost their costumes, music and script.

This idyllic seaside scene is in sharp contrast to the images conjured up by recognition of the postmark on the postcard it was taken from – August 4th, 1914 – the day Britain declare war on Germany and the beginning of the First World War.

c.1915 A steam train travelling along the coast, past the Pier, would take the mail on board a little further along, not having stopped at Colwyn Bay Railway Station just a short distance before this view. In early advertising for the Pier, visitors were encouraged that they may "step from the station platform by means of a most convenient slip footway, almost to the Pier entrance, the distance being only a few yards. And yet it is just far enough to be free from all unpleasant noise."

c.1907. The pier entrance showing an advertisement for Riviere's Grand Orchestra concerts. The Pier was entered from a forebay opposite the main approach to the new Promenade. Ticket offices were situated right and left of the entrance, to control the turnstiles and entrance gates. Each side of the Pier was lit with electric lamps.

On March 27th, 1922 the Pavilion building was completely destroyed by fire, suffering some £40,000 worth of damage, but the fire brigade were able to save the Pier apart from the area immediately near the Pavilion. The entire contents of the Pavilion were lost.

Colwyn Bay's second Pavilion building – seating only 1,350 – had its official opening on July 23rd, 1923, when, following the ceremonial opening by Councillor Joseph Dicken, Chairman of the Pier and Entertainments Committee, and a reception and banquet at the Metropole Hotel, a Grand Gala night concert was held.

The Urban Council bought the Pier in September 1922 and organised the building of the new Pavilion, spending close to £45,000 on the purchase, the building of the new Pavilion and maintenance and renewal of the Pier. Under the supervision of Mr. W. J. Dunning, Council engineer, Messrs. Braithwaite & Co., promised the new Pavilion would be completed by July 23rd and were true to their word.

Sadly, the second Pavilion suffered the same fate as the first and was destroyed by fire on May 16th, 1933. The alarm was raised around 12.30am and once again the fire brigade found a Pavilion too well ablaze to be saved but through concentrating their work on the Pier structure were able to save it once more.

This view of Colwyn Bay Pier and Promenade was taken around August 1933 as both the Pavilion and Bijou Theatre are missing. The Pavilion was lost to fire on May 16th and the Bijou Theatre on August 3rd.

This, the third and present Pavilion was officially opened on May 8th, 1934. The Pavilion had accommodation for between 700 and 750 people in the auditorium, and a special floor for dancing flanked by a spacious café and lounge. This aerial view of the present Pavilion building is from the late 1950s.

An early 1930s view, repairs are carried out to the Pier boardwalk. The Bijou Theatre can be seen at the Pierhead and the second Pavilion building is on the right. The Bijou Theatre burnt down on July 28th, 1933 and was never replaced.

The official opening of this, the third Pavilion, by Councillor W. G. Knowlson, Council Chairman, on May 8th, 1934. The Council's Surveyor Mr. W. G. Dunning, in collaboration with Professor Adshead and Council entertainments manager Louis Kilkenny designed the £16,000 Pavilion building. Having been officially opened the Pavilion opened to the public on May 19th, 1934 with a special holiday attraction – Ernest Binns and his company "Bits and Pieces" in their smart vaudeville entertainment.

Colwyn Bay Corporation's Promenade Omnibus Service buses parked at the Pier entrance. The two on the left are Guy Wolf buses – BDA 41 was in service between 1937 and 1960 and EUN 396 between 1948 and 1960. The Bedfords on the right were to remain in service well into the 1960s.

The Riviére Orchestra. Jules Prudence Riviére was a veteran and world-renowned conductor, known as "chef d'orchestre". He regularly conducted the orchestra that bore his name, with the intention that "he would bestow on Colwyn Bay a musical fame at least equal to what he had previously conferred on Llandudno". M. Riviére died suddenly on December 26th, 1900 (he was 81 years old), and was buried at Llandrillo-yn-Rhos Churchyard, where he is also commemorated in a window of the Church. The Riviére Orchestra retained his name and continued to perform twice daily at the Victoria Pier.

During the holiday season the Pier Orchestra would be kept busy throughout the week – as witnessed by this 1938 advertisement.

PIER PAVILION
COLWYN BAY
Telephone 2594

July to October
RESIDENT SUPER CONCERT PARTY
Nightly at 8.

ORCHESTRAL CONCERTS
Daily at 11 a.m. and 3 p.m.   Sundays at 3 and 8 p.m.
LEADING LONDON ARTISTES
are engaged for the Sunday Concerts.
SPECIAL HOLIDAY PROGRAMMES at EASTER and WHITSUNTIDE

DECK GAMES

BEACH CHALETS:
(NEAR DINGLE—WEST OF PIER).
For Hire by the week—

| JUNE, 12 6 to 17 6 | AUGUST, 20,- to 27 6 |
| JULY, 15/- to 20/- | SEPT., 15/- to 20.- |

Apply Entertainments Manager, The Pier.

In 1968 the council sold the Pier, seen here in the 1980s, to a private company called First Leisure and the Pavilion soon became the Dixieland Showbar, and the Golden Goose Amusements were built at the entrance. It was later sold again, this time to Parker Leisure but was soon closed.

The Pier and Pavilion stood empty and fell into a state of disrepair for many years before it was bought in 1995 by Michael and Ann Paxman, who continue their valiant efforts to restore the Pier to its former glory, with the support of volunteers.

Catlin's famous Pierrots entertained visitors on the Colwyn Bay Hotel side of the Pier around 1907.

Catlin's Arcadia, a more substantial stage, than the one shown above was buillt around 1910. "The Great Showman", Will Catlin (1872-1952) was born in Leicester, his real name being William Henry Fox.

Catlin's
Pierrots
c.1910

Visitors to Colwyn Bay in 1937 were encouraged during their stay to see Ernest Binns' Colwyn Follies – "North Wales' best concert party" – at the Pier Pavilion nightly at 8.00 p.m. The programme changed every Monday and Thursday. Admission (including tax and pier toll) was 2/- and 1/6 for reserved seating, 1/- for unreserved and half price for children under 14.

Catlin's Pierrots at Colwyn Bay in 1911. From left to right, back row: Robert Turley, tenor; Leslie Harold, comedian; W.E. Rouselle, baritone; front row: Will Harris, comedian; Charles Kay, comedian; Reggie Belmont, pianist; Edwin Rose, vocalist; Albert Lyon, singer and dancer.

The most famous concert party to appear in Colwyn Bay were Harry Reynolds' Minstrels. Harry Reynolds' Royal Serenaders were in Colwyn Bay for their 8th season in 1909. Such was the popularity of Harry Reynolds' entertainers that as early as 1902-1903 a "Memoir of Mr. Harry Reynolds' Colwyn Bay Minstrels" had been composed by W. Lloyd Evans, The Postman Poet, having been requested by a large number of visitors and residents of Colwyn Bay. A copy of the memoir could be bought for one penny.

Harry Reynolds' association with Colwyn Bay began almost with the beginning of the 20th century. His working life had begun at 12 years of age in varied work, but a visit to a Minstrels show in London was to seal his fate – he immediately set about organising his own entertainment troupe – carrying out varied tasks from musical director to principal comedian to bill-poster in those early days. As well as seafront entertainment, by 1910 he was also showing Harry Reynolds' "Fabulous Animated Pictures" at the Public Hall in Colwyn Bay. Both entertainments would be combined at the Hall on wet nights. The Royal Serenaders' 1910 season began with an inaugural "Grand Evening Concert" at the Hall, with a new and brilliant programme, including a special display of "Animated Pictures", they then commenced their Alfresco Entertainments on the Promenade at 11, 3 and 7.45 daily. On May 30th, 1910, for one week, a "splendid production of the Funeral of King Edward VIII, and a dozen other interesting pictures" were shown at the Public Hall.

A late 19th century view of Colwyn Bay's new promenade looking east towards Old Colwyn.

A typical scene on a summer's day at the beach in Colwyn Bay during the 1930s.

Old Colwyn Station and viaduct c. 1905. Colwyn Station's first appearance in Bradshaw's Railway Guide was in 1849. The Station was closed in November 1952 despite local protests.

Old Colwyn Promenade c. 1910.

A view of the Promenade in Old Colwyn in 1924, these young charges, in the care of their nannies, were clearly expected to take a constitutional in the sea air, which was so strongly recommended for good health by the medical men of the time due to the mildness and dryness of the local climate.

Unidentified bathers on the jetty with the original Victoria Pavilion in the background. c.1920.

Looking west along the beach towards Rhos-on-Sea in the 1880s, the Colwyn Bay Hotel is clearly visible in the distance along with Gilbertville, the building where Penrhos College began in 1880.

The beach before the promenade. This shows the Colwyn Bay Hotel in the distance, one of the first buildings in what was otherwise a sparsely inhabited area. What became "the Promenade" was originally known as "the Parade".

The new promenade at Rhos-on-Sea. Once constructed, this facilitated the "exercising of carriages" along the Marine Drive in the direction of the Little Orme. The development of the Promenade began in 1872 and continued well into the 20th century. A 1946 official record documents the following lengths of Promenade: Rhos – 330 yards, Rhos to the West Promenade – 920 yards, West Promenade – 480 yards, Colwyn Bay Hotel to the Railway Station – 285 yards, the Railway Station to the Marine Path – 1470 yards, the Marine Path to Old Colwyn – 840 yards, a total of 4325 yards or 2 and a half miles.

F. J. Tucker & Son, Builders and Contractors' trucks lined up along the Cayley Promenade. Tucker & Son were based in what became known as Tucker's Yard, in a lane off Brompton Avenue. Tucker's were one of several businesses working from lock-up garages here, the buildings having been stables at one time.

Marine Road's junction with the West Promenade around 1902. The building immediately behind the shelter is now Toad Hall Inn.

A view of Rhos-on-Sea beach and pier. Rhos-on-Sea was described early in the 20th century as a curious little resort, one mile west of Colwyn Bay, with a beach which "benefits by not being overlooked by the Railway" !

The Colwyn Bay & Liverpool Steamship Company, Ltd.
Registered Office: RHOS-ON-SEA, Colwyn Bay.
The New, Fast, Cross-Channel Saloon Paddle Steamer.

DAILY SERVICE

S.S. RHOS COLWYN

· BETWEEN ·
LIVERPOOL,
COLWYN BAY,
LLANDUDNO
· AND ·
MENAI STRAITS.

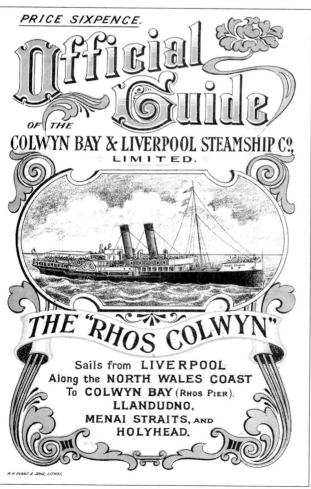

PRICE SIXPENCE.

Official Guide

OF THE

COLWYN BAY & LIVERPOOL STEAMSHIP Cº.,
LIMITED.

THE "RHOS COLWYN"

Sails from LIVERPOOL
Along the NORTH WALES COAST
To COLWYN BAY (RHOS PIER).
LLANDUDNO,
MENAI STRAITS, AND
HOLYHEAD.

W.H. EVANS & SONS, LITHOS.

RHOS COLWYN: The Colwyn Bay and Liverpool Steamship Company's pleasure steamer Rhos Colwyn was certified by the Board of Trade to carry 777 passengers. It performed a regular service to Colwyn Bay (Rhos Pier), Llandudno, Menai Straits, Holyhead, Southport, Blackpool and other ports. Described as a beautifully modelled saloon pleasure passenger steamer, with all modern requirements for the comforts and convenience of the travelling public. The 225 foot vessel was launched in 1900, it had 3 decks, lower, main and promenade, the latter extended the full width of the steamer, the first class saloon occupied a third of the vessel's length on the main deck, upholstered in crimson velvet, woodwork of solid oak, tastefully panelled with cornices in gold. The catering department was described as being a special feature of the steamer, and it seems "good catering, supplemented by attention, civility and good company make a sea trip a pleasurable memory".

Built in Douglas, Isle of Man, in 1869, then dismantled and rebuilt in Rhos-on-Sea in 1895, Rhos Pier was situated at Rhos Point. The Pier was 1,500 feet long and was used by passenger steamers to land passengers. The view looking inland from the pier-end was said to be magnificent.

Over the years Rhos Pier fell into a serious state of disrepair, it was bought by the council in January 1953, but continued to deteriorate. A portion of the Pier is shown here washed up on the promenade in 1954 after being badly damaged by a storm, what was left was demolished soon after.

An all too familiar view of the promenade in Rhos-on-Sea right up to and during the time the Breakwater was built in 1982-83. Work on the Breakwater had begun in late May 1982 but as the North Wales Weekly News described it at the time, this was "Rhos-Under-the-Sea" again at the end of the month.

The £1 million Breakwater project was undertaken by Amey Roadstone Construction, and required the use of special Dutch barges, as seen here, to bring their 600-ton cargos of armour stone as close to the beach as possible so they could then be lifted into position by a large mechanical grab. The cargo was released from underneath the barge as shown here.

In June 1982, one of these Dutch barges, seen here near Rhos Point at low tide, ran aground having been caught up in the load it had just delivered. It became a tourist attraction for the few days it took for tugs to release it.

Completed by June 1983, the Breakwater suffered delays caused by several of the barges becoming caught in the cargo they'd just delivered, and a shortage of armour stone. The use of the barges was discontinued in January 1983, permission having been given by the council for a maximum of 20 loads a day to be transported by road from Mold.

The 500-tonne, Honduras-registered, coaster Marga Cortes ran aground at Rhos-on-Sea on September 29th, 1991, causing considerable damage to the jetty and becoming an instant tourist attraction. The ship had been on its way to Llanddulas to collect a cargo of rocks but was caught up in a storm and holed, spending two days at Rhos beach instead, before it freed itself and departed for offshore repairs in Anglesey.

This clearly shows the Central Hotel which was originally called the Station Hotel, it would have been visible across an open field from the station. It also shows the gas lamp standard presented in 1895 by John Porter, the town's principal architect.

1911. Staff outside the Domestic Bazaar Co. Ltd, next door to Gwalia Chambers, and on the other side was Kinmel House, which became Boots the chemist.

1927. Note Frank Arundale's on the right advertising as a fish and game dealer. Between the Savoy Café and the Central Hotel were the buildings known as the Central Chambers.

Boots the chemist can be seen on the left of the picture, and the spire of St. John's Methodist Church (then the St. John's Wesleyan Church) in the distance. Note the ornate wrought ironwork on the right, which was such a feature of this part of Conway Road.

On the left of this view is the North and South Wales Bank on the corner of Woodland Road West. Originally built in the 1880s it was re-modelled in an Italianate style in 1903-4 by architects Woodfall and Eccles, and today is home to the town's HSBC branch. The original name can still be seen on the bank's outer wall. J. R. Jones' Lancaster House can be seen opposite.

1908. Pryce Williams & Co. on the corner of Penrhyn Road, it became E. B. Jones & Co. Grocers. The Domestic Bazaar can be seen on the left of the picture.

John Homan, the Regent, Conway Road.

1920s advertisement for John Homan's shop on the corner of Llewelyn Road, and their other shops in the town.

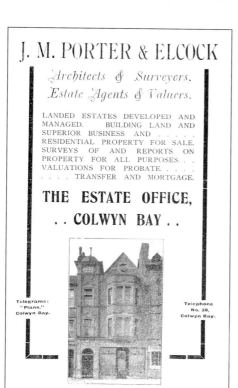

J. M. Porter & Elcock's Estate Office in 1910. Their business was conducted above T. H. Jones' shop, shown below. The building is now the home of Mayfair ladies fashion and bridal wear shop.

A 1920s advertisement for T. H. Jones, Fashionable Hosier and Outfitter.

Colwyn Bay's Town Hall, at Conway Road's junction with Coed Pella Road, opened in 1904 and the War Memorial was erected in 1922. The town's Fire Station was next door. A World War I tank stood beside the Town Hall from 1920 until 1937. The last meeting was held here in March 1964 before the council's move to Glan-y-Don Hall, this building was demolished soon after.

Unveiled on November 22nd, 1922 by Lord Colwyn, the town's War Memorial to those who fell in the Great War is of an infantryman in 1914-18 battledress. Paid for by public subscription, the bronze sculpted by John Cassidy of Manchester was cast by Messrs. H. H. Martyn & Co. of Cheltenham, and stands on a column of Portland Stone cut to a design by Mr. W. J. Dunning, council engineer and surveyor. The War Memorial was sited in front of the Council Offices on Conway Road until their demolition and was then moved to its present site at Rydal Gardens in 1972.

The unveiling, on Armistice Day November 22nd, 1922, of Colwyn Bay's War Memorial to the 173 men and one woman (Catherine Williams of the Queen Alexandra's Imperial Military Nursing Service) lost during World War I was witnessed by a large gathering. On the same day memorial tablets and two memorial windows were unveiled at St. Paul's Church. Both windows were presented by Dinglewood School, one being in memory of the Old Boys of the school who were lost.

Councillor E. A. Neill, chairman of the Welcome Home Fund, makes a short speech before the Mayor unveils the name panels added to Colwyn Bay's War Memorial of those lost during World War II. Eighty-eight names were added at this time, including one woman – Phyllis Nuttall.

Bronderw, built in 1877, is still listed as one of the largest buildings of the town, listed in 1914 as being the home of the Young Men's Christian Association (YMCA).

It is recorded that the local council provided the building with free electricity and gas supplies when it was taken over and used as the "Colwyn Bay British Red Cross Auxiliary Military Hospital" in 1915.

Below: A "toast-rack" tram, no. 21, in front of the Town Hall, in the 1950s.

An early 20th century view of Conway Road – looking from the bottom of Llewelyn Road towards West End. The English Presbyterian Church, opened in 1891, can be seen on the right.

Above: St. John's Methodist Church was known originally as St. John's English Wesleyan Church. The official stone-laying ceremony took place in 1882 and the building was completed in 1888. The builder was Edward Foulkes. Built almost completely of local stone, its spire and lychgate were described as "architectural beauties". At one time there were two services on a Sunday morning, the first for Penrhos College and then the ordinary service that was attended by Rydal pupils.

Above left: Conway Road in the 1880s. Colwyn Bay's first Presbyterian Church was built opposite the bottom of Woodland Road West on the corner of Station Road. Sir John Pender, M.P., gave the land on condition that English services as well as Welsh would be held there. Designed by architect John Douglas of Chester and built by Abel Roberts of Llandudno at a cost of a little over £700 the church could seat a congregation of 200. The Rev. E. W. Evans, M.A. accepted the pastorate in May 1873. In 1879 the Welsh congregation moved across the road to the new Engedi Chapel on Woodland Road West, leaving the Conway Road building to the English congregation. An offer of £1,800 for the building in 1879 was accepted and plans for a new church were made – the English Presbyterian Church opened on the corner of Hawarden Road in 1891.

J. O. Jones, Brompton Stores, stood next door to the council school on Conway Road West in the 1920s. This Family Grocer and Provision Merchant ensured that "all orders entrusted will receive prompt attention".

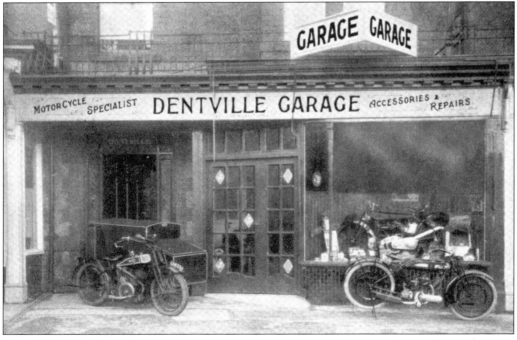

Dentville Garage, the motorcycle specialist for accessories and repairs, was in the row of shops between Brompton Avenue and Prince's Drive in the 1920s. Henry Williams' West End Boot Repairing Depot was next door.

Having traded at several addresses in Colwyn Bay since the early years of the 20th century, perhaps the best remembered business address of J. Fred Francis & Sons was this one at West End, on the corner of Prince's Drive, which opened in the early 1920s.

A 1926 advertisement for the recently opened Conway Road Garage (still fondly spoken of today as Francis Garage) owned by J. Fred Francis and Sons. Remaining a garage over the years though through several name changes, including Gordon Ford, Cowie Ford and finally K. J. Ford before the building was demolished as the 20th century drew to a close. A new Lidl store now awaits an opening date here.

Conway Road Garage

J. FRED FRANCIS & SONS, LTD.

GARAGE FOR PRIVATE CARS
ALL REPAIRS AND PAINTING
Telephone   Five Hundred

Agents for	GREY DE LUXE COACHES	Our Aim :
Alvis,	(Pneumatic Tyres)	To give
Fiat,	HEAD BOOKING OFFICE :	Service
Trojan,	PENRHYN ROAD	and
Lea Francis	SUB-OFFICES AT	Satisfaction
	RHOS AND OLD COLWYN	
	Telephone : 500	

Appointed R.A.C. & A.A. Repairers

On the corner of Queen's Drive, the road on the right, was a house called "Plas Isaf" which was the Misses Everett's Ladies School. By 1914 the house was split into apartments, but by 1925 was the offices of the Liberal Club, who had moved from a building on the corner of Woodland Road East and Abergele Road which was demolished to make way for Woolworths' store.

The corner of Abergele Road and Wynnstay Road, seen here in 1924, before the building was reconstructed to a design by architect Sidney Colwyn Foulkes.

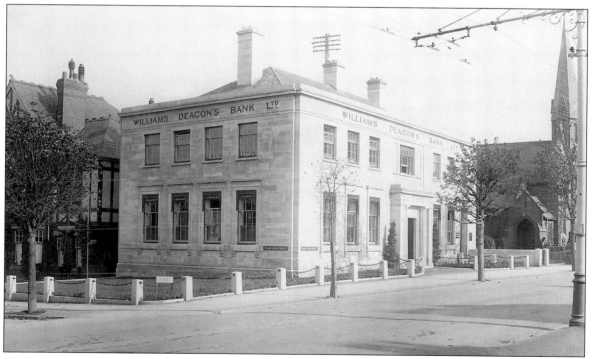

Seen here in 1925, the building was reconstructed for the Williams Deacon's Bank Ltd, later the Williams & Glyn's Bank, now the Royal Bank of Scotland.

The English Presbyterian Church on the corner of Conway Road with Hawarden Road. The site for the church was secured in 1890, designed by architect A. W. Smith of Manchester, and built by Samuel Parry of Llanrwst the foundation stones were laid by Mr. G. W. Taylor of Wrexham, Edward Jones the Mayor of Pwllheli, the Rev. Thomas Parry and John Porter of Pwllycrochan Hotel. Principal Thomas Charles Edwards, D.D. of the University College of Wales, Aberystwyth, opened the church, built of Ruabon brick, on January 11th, 1891.

Conway Road and Hawarden Road. C. 1905. Barclays Bank now occupies the building on the corner.

An advertisement from 1921 for E. B. Jones & Co. on the corner of Penrhyn Road. The shop was previously William Pryce & Co.'s West End Stores but by 1914 was E. B. Jones and remained so until the 1970s.

Briggs and Company, at the corner of Conway and Penrhyn Roads. Their advertising during the early 1900s: "IF IT'S NEW WE HAVE IT !" "there is no importunity to purchase. Call and handle the Finest Footwear produced: The 'Metropole' and 'Wayfarer' Brands". The Briggs shop moved to new premises in Station Road in 2002.

Davies Brothers, 3 Doughty Buildings, Conway Road, in the 1920s. This was an old established business which enjoyed a constant patronage among the fashionable residents, it had a wonderful shop front, enjoying a commanding position and it was said that "every joint leaving the premises was of the best meat and guaranteed perfectly sound, well-fed and in prime condition".

A very busy turn of the century view of the Central Hotel, Livery Stables and Coaching Office. The coach standing on the left of the photograph is outside the Colwyn Bay Coaching Establishment. The policeman and gentleman standing together appear most interested in the photographer.

J. R. Jones, Saddler and Harness Maker, showing an amazing array of leather goods. This shop, having previously been next door but one to the Public Hall, by 1911 had moved back to Abergele Road, this time opposite the Public Hall, continuing to be called Lancaster House.

J. R. Jones, LANCASTER HOUSE, CONWAY ROAD, COLWYN BAY,

Saddler, Collar, Harness and Trunk Maker.

Ladies' and Gentlemen's Riding Saddles.

Boys' and Girls' Pilches.

Driving, Hunting, Riding, and Watering Bridles.

Driving, Riding, Cart & Dog Whips, and Hunting Crops, and all the general lines connected with the trade.

CARRIAGE, GIG, VAN AND CART HARNESS always in Stock, and Made to Order.

A good assortment of Trunks, Dress Baskets, Square and Brief Bags; Dress Suit, Bonnet and Hat Cases. Latest Styles always in Stock. Lowest Prices.

Best Assortment of Dog Collars, Leads and Whips.

Note Address:

LANCASTER HOUSE, CONWAY ROAD,

(New Premises Next The Mews).

A 1904 advertisement for J. R. Jones' business.

Edwin Jones' livery stable at the Mews on Conway Road, (next door to the Central Hotel and opposite the HSBC bank) c. 1895. By the early 20th century these were the business premises of J. Fred Francis.

This 1904 advertisement for J. Fred Francis Coaches (successor to Edwin Jones) details the itinerary for their varied coach tours of north Wales. An early description of one of the tours advertised by this "motor and coaching" firm tells us that "the Tourist" leaves the Mews, Colwyn Bay at 10am prompt, on undoubtedly the finest coaching tour in north Wales, and probably the most popular. The well appointed new Patent Coach proceeded directly to Betws-y-Coed, through the Vale of Conway arriving at the Waterloo Hotel at 12.15 (when luncheon would be ready), then horses having been changed, the coach left at 1.15 sharp via Swallow Falls. Keeping to the Holyhead Road, proceeded to Bethesda, where another change of horses is made." The tour eventually returned at 6.30. Fare 10 shillings each (box seats 2 shillings extra).

What a difference 10 years can make! The above advertisement dates from 1911 and the bottom one from 1921, by which time J. Fred Francis & Sons were occupying their new premises at West End, Colwyn Bay.

Llyfrgell Rydd y Coroniad, Coronation Free Library. A plaque in the porch marks the occasion of the opening: "This library has been built to commemorate the coronation of King Edward VII (August 9th, 1902). The movement for its erection was inaugurated at a town's meeting held April 11th, 1902. The cost of the land and building was defrayed by public subscription, assisted by the generosity of Mr. Andrew Carnegie, who contributed £3,800. The building was opened on April 24th, 1905 by the Rev. Thomas Parry, J.P., C.C., Chairman of the Executive Committee, and this tablet was unveiled by the Rev. J. G. Haworth".

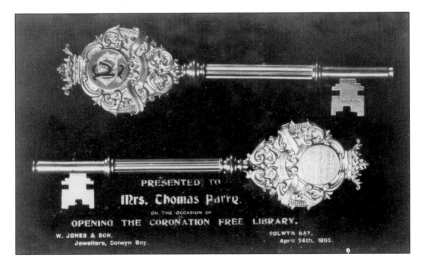

The library building is shown here in 1905. A Children's Library was opened in December 1933 and the Welsh Reference Library opened on March 1st, 1949, having received a donation from the Royal National Eisteddfod of 1947. The Duke of Gloucester laid the Foundation Stone for extensions to the building on June 8th, 1960 and Sir Ben Bowen Thomas, M. A., Permanent Secretary to the Welsh Department of the Ministry of Education, opened the extensions on June 1st, 1962.

The magazine room on the first floor seen shortly after the Library opened in 1905. This room, which has changed remarkably little since the time of the photograph, is currently used as an exhibition gallery.

The Library's exhibition stand at the Pier Pavilion during the 1960s. Librarian Rev. Ivor Davies is accompanied by assistant Hilary Williams (neé Gee). Mr. Davies was Librarian from 1932 until 1962.

Council Officers: The Mayor of the Borough of Colwyn Bay in 1962/3, Councillor William Fox, wearing his mayoral chain, with senior members of council staff. Town Clerk Geoffrey Edwards is to the left of the Mayor, and newly appointed Borough Librarian William R. Flint is standing just behind and slightly to the left of the Town Clerk.

The opening of the 1964 Denbighshire Arts Society Exhibition. In attendance are, from left to right, Nan Pritchard, Borough Librarian William R. Flint, Margaret Flint and Jack French. Mr. Flint became Borough Librarian in September 1962, becoming Area Librarian for Colwyn in the local government reorganisation of 1974. Mrs. Flint was also a long-standing member of staff at Colwyn Bay Library. William Flint retired in December 1980, and sadly passed away in April 1995.

The Library's Treasure Hunt winners receiving their prizes in September 1989. The winners are, from left to right, Richard Evans, Thomas Watson, Richard Watson, Siân Roberts and Ellen Roberts.

The original Ship Inn stood at the top of Church Road, in front of the vicarage. Built in 1736, it was demolished in 1874. The present Ship Hotel was built on the opposite side of Llandudno Road.

Ednyfed Fychan, a chieftain of the 12th century, originally built Llandrillo Church; it is built of stone and consists of 2 aisles and a large square tower, with double stepped battlements and a turret at one corner. Ednyfed's Chapel is said to have formed the western half of the present north aisle, and it is likely that Ednyfed's pew stood in the north side of the aisle. An Arundale's delivery cart can be seen in the foreground. In recent years the outer walls of the Church have been whitewashed.

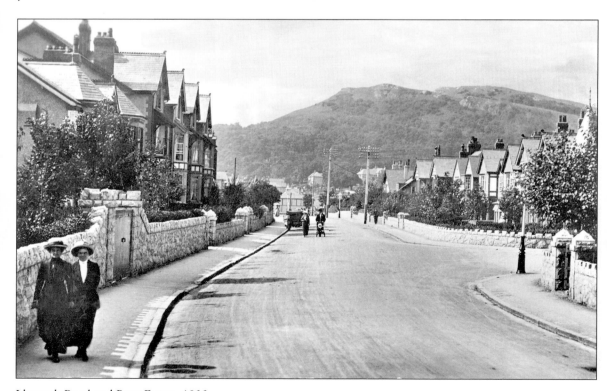

Llanerch Road and Bryn Euryn, 1932.

Bryn Euryn, c. 1926. Situated a little over a mile from Colwyn Bay, Bryn Euryn is described in early guides as an "ancient fortified post". On its lower slopes are the ruins of Llys Euryn, the ancient dwelling place of Ednyfed Fychan, who was chancellor to Llewelyn the Great (and whose tombstone is in Llandrillo Church).

Bryn Euryn from St George's Road, 1926.

The Elwy Road Housing Estate, built during the late 1950s, covers 18 and a half acres. Designed by Sidney Colwyn Foulkes, F.R.I.B.A., when completed it comprised 144 x 3-bedroom houses, 4 x 4-bedroom houses, 30 x 1-bedroom flats and 60 x 2-bedroom flats. The estate, when built, was considered to have several rather unusual features, including castings of characters from the "Alices" and "Edward Lear" over front doors, and canopies painted in coloured stripes protecting these. Different pastel shades of lime wash in the Welsh tradition were used for each house. This view from the air shows the long terraces and the lanes for service access behind the houses.

The Elwy Road Housing Estate, c. 1958.

Two views of the properties built during the 1910s by architects Messrs. Pearce and Moss as they sought to establish a Garden City within Rhos-on-Sea. Their bartering with the local council over the cost of bringing mains gas to their new houses makes for interesting reading as they sought time and again to have their contribution to the costs reduced.

Rhos=Green Garden City

Corner of Abbey Road and Marine Drive,

RHOS-ON-SEA, COLWYN BAY.

Artistic————

Comfortable Houses

SUITABLE FOR . . . .
HOLIDAYS OR RESIDENCE.

Special Plans to each Customer,

Embodying Individual Tastes.

Prices from £350 upwards.

For full particulars apply to the Architects :

SYDNEY MOSS, A.R.I.B.A.,

Tel. 2751 City.   4, St. Ann Square, Manchester

JOSEPH PEARCE,

Royal Insurance Buildings, Liverpool

Tel. 124 Central.

This advertisement for the Rhos Green Garden City development appeared in the Royal National Eisteddfod Official Programme for 1910 when the Eisteddfod visited Colwyn Bay.

Rhos Road, c.1905.

Looking up Rhos Road from the Promenade around 1955.
On the left can be seen J.A. Reynolds' ladies hairdressing salon and R. W. & E. Cole's shop comprising a
tobacconists, confectioners, stationers, fishing tackle and toy store all in one.

Rhos Road, c. 1910.

Trillo Avenue, 1916.

Mrs. G. Roberts ran this specialist footwear shop on Rhos Road, seen here during the 1920s. The shop was known as the Piccadilly Shoe Stores.

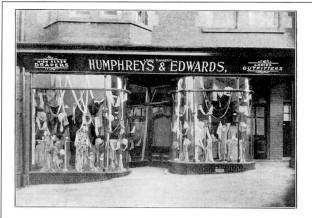

Frank Turner, costumier and draper, was in business next door to the Midland Bank on Rhos Road during the 1920s.

R. F. DAVIES

FAMILY GROCER

PROVISION MERCHANT &
ITALIAN WAREHOUSEMAN

Noted House for
TEAS, COFFEES & Prime Danish BACON

Danish House, Penrhyn Avenue
RHOS-ON-SEA

R. F. Davies' grocery and provisions shop at Danish House during the 1920s was on the left side of Penrhyn Road as you walked from the Promende end, next door to the Utility Buildings.

The recently demolished Rhos County Garage, which stood on a site that was once a busy shipbuilding yard, was advertised in 1926 as "the largest garage on the North Wales coast", and under entirely new management, having been rebuilt and had extensive additions made. "Situated in the centre of Rhos-on-Sea and within two minutes' walk of all the leading Hotels and Boarding Establishments, it offers to the Visitors and Resident every modern convenience. Three large entrances in Penrhyn Avenue, Colwyn Avenue, and Colwyn Crescent. Accomodation for Chauffeurs. Sixteen lock-up garages near Garden City, Rhos-on-Sea".

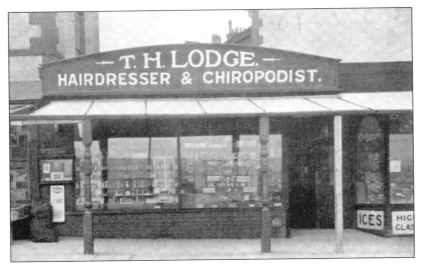

T. H. Lodge, hairdresser and chiropodist, had two local shops during the 1920s. This one on Rhos Road, which was on the right as you entered the road from the Promenade, and one at "The Westminster" on Rhiw Road in Colwyn Bay, which is now the Uniqui needlecraft shop.

Joseph Barnes' shop on Rhos Promenade during the 1920s, among the many services offered was that of booking agent for J. Fred Francis and Sons' coach tours.

Mrs. Perkins' Irish Linen Depot was next door to Rhos Pharmacy on Colwyn Avenue.

St. Trillo's Chapel – dates back to the 6th century and is a Holy Well founded by St. Trillo, the Chapel is thought to be the smallest in Britain, the present building being approximately 120 years old.

Another of the many establishments offering a beneficial stay in the area at the turn of the century was the Rhos Hydro on the corner of Abbey Road and Colwyn Avenue. It was advertised in 1904 as being in Colwyn Bay "the new winter and summer resort" and under the medical supervision of Dr. Brooks who had been "on several occasions" in charge of the Swan Hydro, Harrogate.

Geoffrey Edwards records in his book "The Borough of Colwyn Bay, a social history" that the day the swimming pool at Rhos-on-Sea was opened, August 3rd, 1933, the Bijou Theatre on the Pier burnt down. British boxing champion Jack Petersen opened the pool.

Built on Rhos Promenade as a Welsh Calvinistic Methodist Chapel by the Rev. Thomas Parry, he later decided this was not a suitable location for a Chapel and the building was sold.

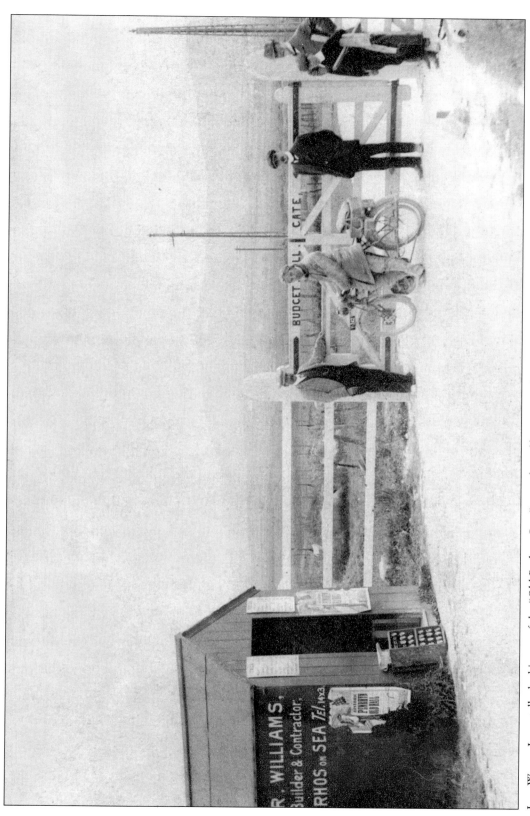

Ivor Wynne Jones tells the history of the "Old Budget Gate" near the golf course on the coast road in "Colwyn Bay, its history across the years". The tollgate was built by landowner William Horton in reaction to David Lloyd George's introduction in 1908 of the Old Age Pensions Act and the tax rises which would follow. The land was sold to the Llandudno and Colwyn Bay Electric Railway Company in 1911, who continued to collect the tolls. Colwyn and Llandudno councils bought the land jointly in 1963 and the collection of tolls ended.

The Ancient Royal Fishing Weir, seen here around 1905, was situated just below the promenade pier in Rhos, it originally belonged to the Cistercian Monks of Aberconwy until they moved to Maenan Abbey. The large triangular enclosure formed of stones and stakes was arranged so that the only way out for water was by a grating at one of its angles, the fish were then caught at low tide.

Rhos Fynach, known as the "marsh farm of the monks", was one of the outlying farms attached to the Abbey at Aberconwy, it not only served as a farm but housed the monks, whose duty it was to fish the weir.

The lady walking towards the buildings is going towards Llandrillo-yn-Rhos Post Office, which occupied the facing building, now a gift shop and café. Glan-y-Mor Cottage was on the right and Rhos Creamery on the left.

HASTEWELL & SMITH

Auctioneers, Architects, Surveyors
House & Estate Agents & Valuers

¶ Particulars of Furnished and Unfurnished Houses for Sale or to Let, post free on application, also Building Plots for Sale or on Lease. Mortgages arranged for.   All classes of Insurance taken. Sales by Auction of Property, Land, Furniture and Effects conducted. Valuations for all purposes, Mortgage, Probate, Fire, &c. Rent Collections and General Management of Property.

Offices : **Rhos Promenade, Rhos-on-Sea**
TELEPHONE 352

Hastewell and Smith's offices in Glan-y-Mor Cottage on the Promenade, near the corner of Rhos Road, seen here in the 1920s.

Lancashire industrialists Brown and Drury opened the Colwyn Bay Hotel in 1871. In 1897 prospective guests were being invited to enjoy seawater baths and avail themselves of the services of the "hotel porters, in scarlet uniform, who attend the trains, and remove luggage to and from the hotel". If this did not entice you to stay then perhaps the final line would: "Colwyn Bay is strongly recommended by eminent medical men for the mildness and dryness of its climate". The hotel was bought by Chester-based Quellyn Roberts & Co. Ltd in 1927.

The Colwyn Bay Hotel had 92 bedrooms and 365 windows – one for each day of the year. Among the many famous guests to stay there were Madame Adelina Patti when she sang at the opening concert at the Pier Pavilion in 1900, ballerina Anna Pavlova, David Lloyd George, pilot Amy Johnson and actor Cary Grant.

During World War Two the Colwyn Bay Hotel became the Ministry of Food's national headquarters and one of 38 premises the Ministry took over as offices and accommodation. The entire food rationing system was organised from Colwyn Bay. The Ministry's emergency messenger system in the form of a pigeon loft was built at the hotel. Although some parts of the Ministry remained in Colwyn Bay until as late as 1956, the Colwyn Bay Hotel was ready to reopen as a hotel again in 1952.

COLWYN BAY HOTEL
TELEPHONE 3345

Following derequisitioning by His Majesty's Government this hotel will be reopening early in 1952, having been modernized and redecorated.

TARIFF WILL BE SENT UPON APPLICATION

A few suites are available

PROPRIETORS : Quellyn Roberts & Co. Ltd., 13 Watergate St., Chester

Having fallen empty and no buyer to be found, the Colwyn Bay Hotel, which had stood proudly on the coastline for over a century, was finally demolished in September 1975.

Princess Court was built on the site of the old Colwyn Bay Hotel. This complex of 128 retirement apartments opened in 1990.

Rhos-on-Sea promenade showing the first Rhos Abbey Hotel.

Built in 1898 and situated near the entrance to Rhos Pier, described in advertising literature as being away from "the dinning noise of the station, and in a bright, breezy and bracing point of the bay", apparently an unrivalled situation! When built this 32-room, brick and half-timbered hotel had grand views ranging over 20 miles of coast and country and was thought to rank amongst the best hotels in Wales. A 15-section stained glass landing window bore the message "Welcome the coming, speed the parting guests."

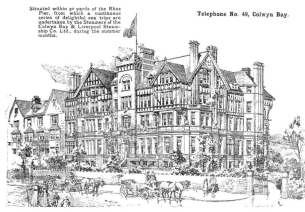

This 1904 advertisement for the Rhos Abbey Hotel included all the "important facts" necessary to make the decision that this was THE hotel at which to stay.

Permission to demolish the hotel was granted in November 2000. Following a public auction of fixtures and fittings in March, by June 2001 the demolition of the Rhos Abbey Hotel had begun.

As the demolition continued apace plans were being put in place for the site to be redeveloped into thirty two-bedroom apartment, and by August 2002 St. Trillo's Court is now well under way here.

The Hydropathic Establishment was built in 1882 to take advantage of Colwyn Bay's growing reputation as a "resort for invalids, particularly those requiring a warm and dry climate". As a Winter Residence it was "recommended by Physicians of the highest eminence on account of its mildness and salubrity" and this building could offer the latest in innovation with its hot air heating system. Charges for services included a 10/6 consultation fee; board, lodging and attendance (including use of baths when prescribed) varied from £2 12s 6d to £3 13s 6d depending on the room. Fire in a private sitting room or bedroom was 1s 6d a day extra or 9d for an evening. The building was acquired by Penrhos College from the Pwllycrochan Estate Company in 1895.

with D'r Shaw's Compts—

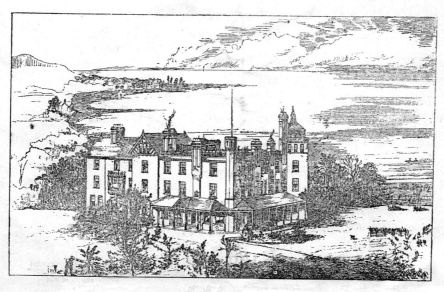

⊱⊰ HYDROPATHIC ⊱⊰ ESTABLISHMENT ⊱⊰

AND WINTER RESIDENCE,

⊱ COLWYN · BAY, · NORTH · WALES. ⊰

𝔐edical 𝔖uperintendent:

THOMAS SHAW, L.R.C.P.

A S it is intended to carry out the Hydropathic treatment as effectively as possible, special attention has been directed to the construction of the Baths.

A great feature of this Establishment is the abundant supply of Seawater throughout the year, which is pumped in direct from the Bay.

Note, please book to Colwyn Bay Station not Colwyn

Use of the baths was available to residents and non-residents alike. The Turkish Baths, at a cost of 2s 6d, were available for gentlemen on Mondays, Wednesdays, Thursdays and Saturdays between 9.00 a.m. and 6.00 p.m., but for ladies only on Tuesdays and Fridays between 9.00 a.m. and 1.00 p.m., and afterwards for gentlemen. Bathing could take place in fresh water or seawater; seaweed or ozone baths were also available.

Penrhos College

COLWYN BAY,

A HIGH-CLASS SCHOOL FOR GIRLS (BOARDERS ONLY). INDIVIDUAL ATTENTION COMBINED WITH THE ESPRIT DE CORPS OF A LARGE SCHOOL.

LADY PRINCIPAL:

MISS HOVEY, B.A. (Lond.)

FOURTEEN RESIDENT MISTRESSES, of whom seven are Graduates, and the others Specialists for Music (four), Art, Gymnastics and French Conversation. Lady Matron, Miss E. M. Hovey.

Fine School and House Buildings, with Botanical and Chemical Laboratories, Studio, Seven other Class Rooms, Music Practising Rooms, Gymnasium, Library and Drawing Room, all for the use of Pupils, Bedrooms for one, two or three girls. Electric Light and perfect Ventilation throughout, Heating Apparatus on all floors. Detached Sanatorium.

The **FOURTEEN ACRES OF GROUND** have a long sea frontage, eleven Tennis Courts, three Hockey Lawns and Basket Ball and Cricket Fields. Physical Exercise also includes general and remedial gymnastics, swimming and riding.

Three **SCHOLARSHIPS,** tenable in the School, or on leaving. Successful preparation for University Entrance and other Examinations.

A small **JUNIOR SCHOOL** is to be opened in a separate building, for girls under 14, in May, 1911.

Left: This advertisement was included in the Royal National Eisteddfod's Official Programme in 1910. Preparations were being made at this time for the addition of a small junior school that would be open by May of the following year.

Right: Gilbertville: Penrhos College was established in this building on the promenade on September 23rd, 1880. The building came later to be known as Gilbertville and was run as a private hotel. The school was named Penrhos College rather than school, as this was the custom for girls' boarding schools of the time. Headmistress Miss Wenn and Matron Miss Martin, assisted by 2 pupil teachers had 12 pupils initially, a number which had increased to 33 by the second term, and 60 by the end of the year. There was no school uniform in these early days.

The "Lady Principal" of Penrhos College from December 1894 until August 1928, Rosa Hovey, B.A. was an old girl of Penrhos College. She oversaw great development and growth during her time in charge, and upon being invited to record the history of the College in a book, the foreword by the Rev. H. Lefroy Yorke on behalf of the governors stated that "had the authorship been submitted to other hands, tribute must, in justice, have been paid to the wise and devoted service rendered by Miss Hovey herself". Following her death a Memorial Service was held at the College on October 21st, 1932, with tribute being paid by the Headmaster of Rydal School, the Rev. A. J. Costain, who concluded "Her work lives after her, and it will live through the years."

The College was founded on strong Wesleyan Methodist principles, initially with the intention of being a School for the daughters of Wesleyan Methodists. Wesleyan Minister Rev. F. Payne was actively involved and became the College's Honorary Secretary. The Rev. Payne was also to raise money to aid the building of St. John's Wesleyan Church, which opened in 1887.

A range of German-made postcards showing views of the college was available to be used by pupils and staff during the early 1900s. This one of a classroom scene was posted in 1902.

Penrhos College from the south-east. During the early years visiting masters arrived by train during the week, to teach mathematics, botany, drawing, music, harmony, class-singing, and callisthenics. Miss Hovey's history of the school records that "the mathematics master was very dark and rather terrifying, and most girls failed to make any progress".

The Penrhos main site in the 1950s, an aerial view from the direction of the Promenade. The railway line runs behind the college, and Allen's Depository can be seen on Prince's Drive. From the time of buying the Hydropathic Establishment until well after the Great War, new buildings were built or land was bought every year – a total of 35 additions in 35 years. Shortly after World War I the school had 350 girls.

Chancellor of the Exchequer David Lloyd-George, accompanied by Mrs. Lloyd-George and daughter Megan, made a speech at the Royal National Eisteddfod in Colwyn Bay and visited Penrhos College in September, 1910, to present prizes and certificates to the successful pupils on Prize Day and also to lay the foundation stone for the new Preparatory School building. Welcomed by Principal Miss Hovey, the Chancellor was himself presented with two gifts before he left the College, the first a silver trowel from Mr. C. Ernest Elcock, of Messrs. J. M. Porter and Elcock, the architects of the new building; the second gift, an ivory mallet, presented by the contractor, Oswald Jones. Jewellers Messrs. W. Jones and Sons of Station Road supplied both gifts.

Seen over the doorway of the Great Hall shown below, are the Penrhos College logo and motto. Semper Ad Lucem translates as "always towards the light".

The Great Hall (the Chapel) was completed in 1925, and was used for daily prayers, assemblies, Sunday Services, lectures and entertainments. The school logo and motto shown above in more detail was over the doorway.

In 1898 the schoolhouse was built, containing the gymnasium fully equipped with fashionable Swedish apparatus, six classrooms, two floors of bedrooms, and six music rooms. The gymnasium entrance was through two doors on the southwest side, to which a porch entrance was added at a later date. Rosa Hovey records in her history of Penrhos 1880-1930 how, for an Old Girls' Reunion in 1898, "A novel entertainment was given when a number of pupils gave a gymnastic display, which was very creditable, and much enjoyed by all who witnessed it."

A view of one of the shared pupil bedrooms in College House at the College complete with very basic sanitary arrangements. By 1914 all bedrooms over the Dining Hall had hot and cold water available. Girls at the College were allowed to receive "stores" or treats, in addition to the plain school fare, which were officially kept in a basement room and access permitted once daily. However the temptation was for the girls to gather together and have midnight feasts, long before midnight, in the bedrooms.

On July 11th, 1980 the Prince of Wales flew in to visit the college; he unveiled a plaque commemorating his visit and the centenary of the school. The pupil numbers for the year was 377 of whom 70 were from overseas.

Headmaster Nigel Peacock (Headmaster from 1974 until 1993) prepares to greet the Prince of Wales during his visit.

With Christmas Greetings.

PENRHÔS COLLEGE, COLWYN BAY.

Ernst R.H.

A Christmas postcard and further views of the College on postcards sent during the early years of the 20th century.

1903

WEST SIDE.
PENRHOS COLLEGE
COLWYN BAY
NORTH WALES.

Darling Ally.
So sorry I carn't find time to answer your dear little letter.
much love
Beat

FRONT VERANDAH.
PENRHOS COLLEGE
COLWYN BAY
NORTH WALES.

Have you got back to school again yet.
Sorry I did at see you
Best love
Beat.

In 1976, the building that had been the Sanatorium was redesigned and reopened as a sixth form house, Beardsworth House, so named in honour of the retiring Deputy Headmistress.

Mary, Duchess of Devonshire, opened the new Chatsworth building, built on the site of the old Physics Laboratory, in October 1957. Leonard Moseley of J.M. Porter and Company was the architect. The Domestic Science Department was on the top floor of this new building. The entire school had been evacuated to Chatsworth House, in Derbyshire, in August 1939, when the Ministry of Food took over the College; they did not return to Penrhos until May 1946.

Rydal Penrhos Girls' Division's final sixth form dinner and toast took place at Penrhos College on the evening of February 24th, 1999. The domestic staff had also prepared a striking cake, bearing the College's motto, to mark the occasion.

Rhian Jones, head cook; Mary Cummings, domestic bursar and Nancy, cook, at the College during 1998/99.

Staff at College during the last Christmas, 1998. Back row, from left to right: unknown, Irene, Janet, Carol, Cath, Mair, Denise, Angela, Dennis, Janet, Elizabeth, Jane, Rhian, Bernadette; front row : Nancy, Debbie, Shirley, Sonia, Tracy.

Above: Once begun in April 2002, the demolition of the buildings on the Penrhos College site continued apace. Plans for the site once cleared are for 99 houses to be built by David McLean Homes of Chester. Local residents opposed earlier proposals for 230 houses, a hotel and an office block on the site.

Above left: Penrhos College and Rydal School merged in 1995 to become Rydal Penrhos. The Penrhos College site became the Rydal Penrhos Girls' Division.

Left: A public auction was held at the College in March 2000, giving former pupils and staff, along with the general public, the opportunity to buy items that would remind them of their time at the College. Demolition of the site began in April 2002.

Chapter 7 - Station Road

A brass band and parade travels up Station Road at the beginning of the 20th century.

Above left: By the 1880s Station Road was able to offer the customer a Post Office, a bank, a boot maker, a grocer and the Daniel Allen store's fine goods. The Maypole Dairy can be seen at the top of the right row of shops, continuing here until the late 1960s, the premises eventually became part of Colwyn House.

Left: A view looking towards the station in the 1930s. Ivor Wynne Jones once described Colwyn Bay's Station Road, in its heyday, as being "a Mecca for north Wales shoppers seeking elegance and quality". John Porter presented the drinking fountain at the top of Station Road to the town on January 17th, 1895, it was removed in 1964 and the policeman who had always directed traffic there also disappeared. Station Road itself eventually became a one-way street in the direction of the station and in 1988 was pedestrianised.

RHYDWEN JONES & DAVIES
"Ye Olde Poste Office"

STATION ROAD - - - COLWYN BAY

TELEPHONE - 67

CABINET MAKERS AND UPHOLSTERERS

*Loose Covers, Curtains &
Draperies our Speciality.*

REMOVERS AND STORERS

ESTIMATES FREE

ALSO AT - - - - RHYL AND LLANDUDNO

Left: A 1921 advertisement for Rhydwen Jones & Davies of "Ye Olde Poste Office", the building having indeed previously been the town's Post Office. This building is one of a row of nine red brick shops built by Edward Foulkes, father of architect Sidney Colwyn Foulkes, on the left side of the road looking towards the station. If you look up towards the top of this building the Post Office name can still be seen in the red brickwork. The business was taken over by Courts in the 1980s and Bewise ladies, mens and children's fashions have traded there for the last 10 years.

Right: Established in 1869, Daniel Allen & Sons moved into premises on Station Road in 1883 to sell the finest furniture, china and carpets, and to provide their services as "funeral furnishers". This advertisement is from 1911. Their shop closed in 1971 and the building was then variously occupied, including a Tomms store and later a Poundstretcher store. During 2002 a new pub called The Litten Tree has opened.

ALLEN & SONS
6 & 7 Station Road, Colwyn Bay

TELEPHONE 197.

Cabinet Makers, Upholsterers
Furniture Removers, Storers
Glass and China Warehouse

DINNER, TEA, AND BREAKFAST SERVICES

SOLE NORTH WALES AGENTS for MESSRS.

Liberty & Co., Ltd.
LONDON.

Below: A 1920s advertisement for J. Dicken & Sons who traded from Queen's Buildings (completed in 1892), next door to the former Municipal Building, they also had a shop in Vaughan Street, Llandudno. As well as furniture sales and removal services they were also Funeral Directors. A New Look fashion store is now in this building.

BEAUTIFUL BRITAIN

THE ARTISTIC HOUSE FURNISHERS

J. DICKEN & SONS
STATION ROAD, COLWYN BAY

ESTABLISHED HALF A CENTURY

STATION ROAD, COLWYN BAY Telephone No. 175
VAUGHAN STREET, LLANDUDNO Telephone No. 5

Cabinet Manufacturers

Complete House Furnishers

Funeral Directors

Removal Contractors & Storers

¶ The Largest, Best and Cheapest House in North Wales for every description of Furniture, Beddings, Linoleums, Curtains, Carpets, Draperies, Bedsteads, China, etc. Perfect Fitting Blinds and Casements, all at Economic Prices.

¶ Estimates for all kinds of Furnishing

The building previously on this site was demolished to enable this still striking building, designed by architect Sidney Colwyn Foulkes, to be built for Mr. W.S. Wood. Colwyn House opened on October 15th, 1935. The building is presently part of the Peacocks chain of clothing stores.

Completed in 1892, the Municipal Building accommodated the National Provincial Bank of England Limited, the Denbighshire County Council, the Colwyn Bay and Pwllycrochan Estate Company Limited and the Colwyn Bay and Colwyn Local Board, as witnessed by the stonework towards the top of the building. In 1901 the Urban District Council's offices were based here. A close look will reveal a pair of handcuffs and the scales of justice in the stonework around the door, a reminder of the time this was the town's first Police Station.

Below: The Andrew Fraser Memorial Clock at the bottom of Station Road. The plaque on the clock reads: "This clock is presented to the people of Colwyn Bay by the parents of Andrew P. Fraser, B.Sc., F.C.A. Born 1st May, 1950, Colwyn Bay. Died 16th February, 1984, Brussels. To commemorate their son's short lifetime during which he achieved so much. A humanitarian, musician, mountaineer and traveller. Time is precious. Erected 8th September, 1989."

A second plaque had also to be added: "This clock is a tribute to the craftsmen of the ancient and venerable firm of J. B. Joyce and Co. of Whitchurch, Shropshire, founded in the year 1690, and especially to Peter Bellingham of Whitchurch who was fatally injured whilst applying his skills with his colleagues on 16th August, 1989."

During the ten days of Christmas every year, this unique clock chimes out a selection of Carols, in each quarter hour. Also, on the 1st May, Andrew's birthday, another selection of melodies throughout the day. "Set for 100 years" say Joyces of Whitchurch, clockmakers.

ESTABLISHED 1879.

London House, COLWYN BAY.

J. O. JONES,

High-Class Drapery Establishment.

EVERY ARTICLE FOR LADIES' ATTIRE.

BLOUSE, COSTUME, COAT, and MANTLE SPECIALIST.

Welsh Shawls—Hundreds to select from.

Millinery, Laces, Ribbons, Gloves & Neckwear of all Descriptions

Dressmaking and Ladies' Tailoring on the Premises.

Above: A 1910 advertisement for J. O. Jones' drapers shop at London House, the building was later occupied by Neville & Co. but demolished in 1979.

Above left: A photograph taken in 1887 from the old station yard looking up Station Road. The Imperial Hotel can be seen on the right and the Central Hotel at the top was then called the Station Hotel. By 1911 the Central Hotel boasted the "finest grill room in Colwyn" and served "Mitchell's and Butler's highest class ales and stouts, wines and spirits".

Left: Looking up a tree-lined Station Road in the 1920s. J. Dicken & Sons' shop can be seen on the right, and London House, the premises of J. O. Jones, on the left. Buckley's Café can be seen on Abergele Road, opposite the top of the road.

Established in 1868, costumiers and drapers Neville & Co. moved into London House after J. O. Jones, and were to become a long established business in Station Road. By 1914 the proprietor was G. J. Parrick. Neville's was "the house for high-class drapery goods at moderate prices", where inspection was invited whether purchasing or not. In 1925 customers were being invited to buy very special value new mercerised cotton foulards in the latest eastern designs and colourings, with the added incentive of free patterns to accompany the fabric purchased. A 1929 advertisement for Jaeger pure wool asked "why sacrifice warmth for daintiness when you can have both by wearing Jaegar underwear? Remember, too – it is replaced if it shrinks." During 1979 the Neville & Co. shop was demolished to make way for the present Boots building.

AGENTS FOR JAEGER
AGENTS FOR ROYAL WORCESTER CORSETS
AGENTS FOR BURBERRY'S

A turn of the century view of Colwyn Bay Railway Station before the expansion of the tracks between the station and Llandudno Junction from two to four in 1904, this was reduced back to two tracks again in 1983.

Colwyn Bay Railway Station and Station Square before redevelopment began in November, 1980. To the right was Victoria Avenue leading to the promenade past Pat Collins' Amusement Park, next to that was the ambulance station. The appearance of this whole area changed when the A55 Expressway was built.

The goods yard opened on March 28th, 1904 on a site that had seen huge quantities of soil being removed during the building of the railway embankment around the 1840s. The tops of the rides at the old Pat Collins Amusement Park on the seaward side of the goods yard can also be seen. The Bay View Shopping Centre now stands on the site of the goods yard and the A55 Expressway passes close by.

The Post Office on Penrhyn Road, c.1904, having previously been on both Conway and Station Roads, and then moving to Princes Drive in 1926. This Post Office building was situated opposite Penrhyn Stores (which was next to the Metropole Hotel). It is interesting to note that the business hours of the Post Office around this time were 7am–9pm on weekdays, 8am–10am on Sundays. There were three deliveries on a weekday and one on a Sunday!

An early 20th century view of Penrhyn Road. Halfway down on the right-hand-side are the original premises of W. H. Smith & Son, other shops included Penrhyn Pharmacy (chemist – Mr. E. A. Neill, M.P.S.), Mills & Son – house furnishers, Portland House – which was a ladies' and children's outfitters and Briggs and Sons on the corner of Penrhyn Road and Conwy Road.

The Lantern Cafe

Penrhyn   Road
Colwyn   Bay

———

Morning Coffee
Teas and Ices

———

ALWAYS OPEN
LATE

Above right: A view down the right hand side of Penrhyn Road c. 1929. Among the shops that can be seen here are Herbert Tomkinson's printers and stationers (also shown below right); the Hygienic Creameries in Strand House next door; A. J. Fleet & Sons' music warehouse (who were tuners for both Colwyn Bay and Llandudno Pier Pavilions); Madame Grey's ladies and children's outfitter in Portland House, and the Penrhyn Pharmacy at no. 20. Notice the uniformed chauffeur standing beside his vehicle in the centre of the photograph.

Right: Tomkinsons "The Indispensible Printing Works". c. 1920. This shop is now Sheldons Stationers.

Coaches preparing for excursions from outside the Metropole Hotel. The Metropole was built in 1898, and indeed continues to dominate, the lower corner of Penrhyn Road. Those who could afford to after shopping took coffee here. During the Second World War, the Ministry of Food took possession of the Metropole and most other hotels in the town, 38 premises in all. The Metropole became a staff canteen and stayed thus until the end of the war when hotels were returned to their owners, although not all reopened. The ground floor of the Metropole became a restaurant in 1951, with the upper floors kept as government offices. The building is now a housing association apartment complex with the Citizen's Advice Bureau and other offices in the basement.

HOTEL METROPOLE

(UNLICENSED)

A. A.   **COLWYN BAY**
NORTH WALES   R. A. C.

Two Minutes from Promenade and Pier
One Minute from Station

❖

Convenient for Penrhos College and
Rydal School

❖

BEDROOMS with HOT and COLD RUNNING WATER

ELECTRIC FIRES
CENTRAL HEATING ❖ BALL-ROOM
EXCELLENT CUISINE AND SERVICE

Special Winter Terms

TELEGRAMS:
" Metropole, Colwyn Bay "

TELEPHONE:
2888 Colwyn Bay

A 1930s advertisement for the unlicensed Hotel Metropole.

A 1914 advertisement for
Mills & Sons, cabinetmakers.

A 1930s advertisement for
Ambler's, the "favourite café
for morning coffee and dainty
afternoon teas". They also
owned the Premier Café on
Station Road.

A view of Abergele Road from the top of Station Road, during the 1920s. To the right is the National Provincial Bank and Provincial Buildings, now the premises of Nat West Bank.

W. BUCKLEY
CONFECTIONER.

High-class CONFECTIONERY, made from the Best and Purest Materials.

Specialities —

Buckley's
Celebrated
Potted Beef.

Made from the Choicest Fresh Meat.

This speciality has for many years obtained more than local reputation, and is being despatched by post to various parts of the country.

Established 1882.
Telephone No. 40.

Dainty Cakes for Afternoon Teas.

Agent for all the Leading English and Continental Chocolate Manufacturers.

SOLE AGENT FOR LOBECK'S & CARSON'S SWEETS AND CHOCOLATES

Withington House
COLWYN BAY.

No. 2a, Withington House, Buckley's Café for "High-Class Confectionery and Tea-rooms". 1911. Sometimes listed as being part of Conwy Road in early Official Street Directories, this building is now part of the Nat West Bank on Abergele Road.

Waterworth Brothers Fruit Stores at the junction of Abergele Road and Woodland Road West, c. 1910. By 1925 the shop was run by Abel Jones, fruiterer.

In the Official Street Directory for 1929 both Britannia House at no. 12 and Abel Jones' shop at no. 14 – the buildings shown here – were empty, soon to be demolished and replaced by F.W. Woolworth & Co.'s bazaar. W. T. Williams' Central Boot Repairing Company can be seen on Woodland Road East.

Douglas & Fordham designed St. Paul's Church, the nave being built in 1887-8 and the chancel added in 1894-5, other additions continued to be made until 1911. The Vicarage to the right of the photograph and the Church Hall to the left were added in 1895. The congregation originally met in a carpenter's shop, and a previous church building burnt down in 1886.

A more familiar view of St. Paul's Church as we recognise the building today complete with tower, which had been added in 1910-11.

A view of the bottom of Rhiw Road showing the route of the tramway through the town, around 1915.

Abergele Road from the bottom of Rhiw Road looking towards the town, around 1903. Mail continues to be collected from a post box at the bottom of Rhiw Road.

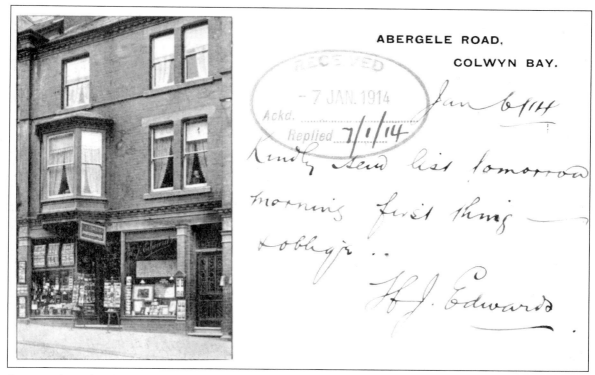

RECEIVED

— 7 JAN. 1914

Ackd.

Replied 7/1/14

Jan 6/14

Kindly send list tomorrow morning first thing & oblige ..

H. J. Edwards

A postcard sent by photographer H. J. Edwards from his office at Carlton House, Abergele Road to J. M. Porter at the Estate Office, Conwy Road, (a distance of 5 minutes on foot) at a cost of a halfpenny, on January 6th, 1914, postmarked 8.45 p.m.

A. Jenkinson and Sons, florist and greengrocer. c1910. The shop, now an antique shop, stands on Rhiw Bank Avenue's junction with Abergele Road.

By January 1915, William Shepherd and Sons of Rochdale were progressing well with the extension of the tramlines along Abergele Road, passing the top of Greenfield Road here and heading towards Old Colwyn. The Victoria Restaurant can be seen on the left and the Midland Garage, later Braids, further along the same side of the road.

The area of Abergele Road between Belgrave Road and Erskine Road opposite the bottom of Grove Park. Meifod House, to the right of the row of shops, was F. W. Sowden's Dairy, next door was Edward Ward, Herbalist, then Madame Heléne, expert palmist at Dingle Dean, with R. Jones the draper on the corner. The area to the right of Grove Park is being redeveloped during 2002, several shops having already been demolished.

This is London House on the corner of Nant-y-Glyn Road and Abergele Road, which is now the Park Hotel; Nant-y-Glyn Methodist Church (not in view) is on the opposite corner. For the first half of the century the building was the business premises of J. K. Williams wine and spirit merchants as seen here, later called Williams Brothers, becoming the Park Hotel during the 1950s.

Colwyn Bay Laundry, Abergele Road, Colwyn Bay

By "MURIEL"

DURING my peregrinations, I recently paid a visit to the above well-known Laundry, and must admit it interested me very much because of the personal note about it. Have you ever been in a Laundry, a modern Laundry, one in the country? If not, this will interest you.

There is not one person in a thousand that knows what has to be done with the shirt or table-cloth after it leaves the house, but you should know, because the shirt and table-cloth are by no means unimportant items to the comforts of life. What happens at a Model Laundry is briefly as follows :— First, the vans arrive with a collection of soiled linen, which is taken to a special building where it is sorted and marked.

Now let us enter the Laundry proper.

Washing machines revolve, cylinders oscillate, full of clothes, being washed with a thoroughness and consistency unobtainable by frail humanity. Whilst observing one of the large washing machines at work (and I incidentally learnt that in this Laundry they employ several of the largest machines made) the Manager stated that some people had queer ideas as to the nature of a washing machine and mentioned that once when showing a certain lady round, had one of the washing machines opened for her inspection ; after looking hard at the smooth bright brass interior of the inner cage holding the linen, the lady exclaimed : "However do they wash? I always thought a washing machine was full of revolving brushes."

The action of cleansing the goods is simply accomplished by the goods falling in the soapy water as they revolve inside the smooth brass cylinder, the dirt coming out with the aid of pure soap, and a good supply of soft water, as if by magic, for the Proprietor insists

upon the use of the very best materials. The hydro-extractor, so different to the ordinary wringer, is one in which the water positively flies out, yet the clothes are not squeezed, nor buttons broken.

Solely for the benefit of customers the Proprietor has added to the Laundry's splendid equipment—already one of the best in these parts—a special process in the washing department which will prolong the life of goods, and at the same time improve the colour and remove all stains without the use of chemicals.

Shirts are ironed with machines, too elaborately constructed to describe, and neckbands made to stand up the right way on a machine for this purpose, but machines cannot do all, for at long tables are rows of healthy girls ironing by hand.

The irons are heated by a mixture of gas and air ; they are always at the same temperature, and thus avoid scorching. No department of work comes in for so much criticism as the dressing of gentlemen's linen.

Starching and blueing is done by machinery, as also the largest sheets and the smallest handkerchief, which leave the revolving rollers aired, glossed, and ready for use.

An up-to-date Laundry's methods always ensure the best possible results, that cannot fail to call forth praise from the most exacting. The result they aim at is that their work shall not only look nice, but feel nice.

To this end they pay special attention to folding, glossing, and removing all chances of irritation especially with collars.

Table linen dressed by them, gives to the dining-room the note of distinction, in fact it is positively appetizing. In another department, garments are being dried; a beautiful, warm, sweet-smelling air pervades it—in fact, an artificial summer breeze.

Surrounding the laundry are extensive drying grounds, where the pure breezes pass through the clothes, and the sweet air has not a little to do with the appearance of the finished articles.

A familiar collection of human garments appear in a division designed to air them, so that you won't catch cold if you put something on straight out of the laundry hamper.

Everything then finds it way to the packing department, for all the world like a miniature G.P.O. Next time your washing arrives, think of this. If you wish your linen to look the thing, send it to this Laundry.

Collection and Delivery

It will no doubt surprise many people to learn that the Colwyn Bay Laundry serves an area of roughly fifty miles' radius, so that should you experience any difficulty respecting the usual Laundry-work in the district you live, please communicate with them, and they will at once advise you as to whether they collect with their own vans or give you the name of their nearest Agent.

They have Agents in all the most important districts of North Wales. Goods received by post are generally placed in hand at once and returned next day if accompanied by remittance. Full list of charges for Laundry work mailed per return on receipt of name and address.

Dyeing and Cleaning

A modern Laundry of any importance is hardly up-to-date unless a department or branch incorporating "Dyeing and Cleaning" is combined with the Laundry.
They undertake all classes of Dyeing and Cleaning, giving you a choice of the latest Art Shades in Colours and quick despatch in Dry Cleaning.

How economical it is to-day (owing to the high prices of new goods) to have an article dyed, almost every lady or gentleman realizes, as either a dress or suit can be dyed so as to look like a new article, and how very different the expenditure.

Dry Cleaning again is quite a present-day feature enabling you to have your favourite Dress or Costume thoroughly cleaned without unpicking no matter what the article is made of, Silk, Wool, or Cotton, or however many varieties of colours.

Carpet Dusting

In connection with Carpet Dusting and Cleaning they have an Electric Carpet Dusting Department, a process that they consider the best possible for freeing any Carpet from dust and grit. The Electric Machine employed will take in the largest Carpets, which after being freed from dust are mechanically brushed by means of revolving brushes. These brushes (although soft enough to place the hand under whilst revolving) quickly raise the pile and impart a clean and fresh look to the Carpets.

Carpets for dusting can usually be returned in an hour or two, also there is no need to wait for a fine day as they are usually dusting Carpets every working day.

Carpet Shampooing

This process many patrons have declared is truly marvellous as regards restoring the Colours of a Carpet and in application is much after the style of a spirit shampoo to the human hair. Full particulars together with list of charges will gladly be forwarded on request.

COLWYN BAY LAUNDRY, Abergele Road, COLWYN BAY
TELEPHONE No. 70

Colwyn Bay and West Denbighshire Hospital. Architect Sidney Colwyn Foulkes' drawing of the proposed new hospital buildings beside the Cottage Hospital in Hesketh Road, during the early 1920s.

Colwyn Bay's Hospital was established in 1897 and opened in 1899 as a Cottage Hospital to commemorate Queen Victoria's Jubilee, with a men's ward and a women's ward each for four patients. As early as July, 1920 plans were being made to transform the Cottage Hospital into the Colwyn Bay and West Denbighshire Hospital, when a "Grand Bazaar and Fete" was held at Queen's Lodge, the home of Lord and Lady Colwyn, to help raise funds. Lord Colwyn is seen here laying the foundation stone for the new hospital buildings, which he officially opened on October 17th, 1925. The cost, including equipment, was about £35,000 and the hospital could then provide for 54 patients.

The Official
Opening of the
Colwyn Leisure
Centre, in Eirias
Park, by Princess
Margaret –
May 12th, 1981.

Princess Margaret greets
the Chief Executive and
Town Clerk Geoffrey
Edwards as she arrives.

The opening
ceremony takes place
as Princess Margaret
accompanied by the
Mayor, Councillor
R.G. Williams,
unveils the
commemorative
plaque.

There followed a tour of the centre – built to accommodate as wide a variety of sports as possible, including archery, badminton, bowls, boxing, cricket, fencing, five-a-side football, gymnastics, basketball, hockey, judo, karate, kendo, lacrosse, lawn tennis, netball, table tennis, trampolining, tug of war, volleyball, wrestling and roller skating along with a swimming pool, lounge and snack bar and facilities to accommodate conferences and meetings. This £1.8 million centre was built by Norwest Holst (Contractors) Limited beginning on February 4th, 1980 and the project was completed on April 16th, 1981.

Built in 1911 as a convalescent home to the design of architect Percy Scott Worthington of Manchester, Glan-y-Don Hall, is seen here before Colwyn Borough Council, purchased it in November 1960, from Cheadle Royal Hospital. Colonel J. C. Wynne Finch, former Lord Lieutenant of the County of Denbigh, officially opened the building as the new Civic Centre on May 14th, 1964.

Right: Windsor House – one of two shops established in Colwyn Bay in 1879 by Messrs. Davies Brothers, "Purveyors of Meat". The other shop was at Doughty Buildings on Conway Road. This shop was on Abergele Road between Belgrave and Erw Wen Roads, next door to Waterworths Brothers fruiters. The proprietors were considered "expert judges of stock" and customers could consider themselves in "perfectly safe hands" should they buy "home-grown and home-fed beef or the little Welsh beauty mutton".

Above right: Eirias Park occupies 52 acres in the centre of the town, between Abergele Road and the promenade. 27 acres were acquired in 1921 and the remainder in 1929. The Four Oaks Restaurant, opened in July 1971, next to the Leisure Centre, was demolished in 2002 having fallen into disrepair over recent years.

Originally known as the Midland Garage, which during World War I manufactured munitions of war here, this property on the corner of Erw Wen Road, was to become Braid Brothers' Automobile Palace. During the 1930s the garage stocked 200 new and used cars and sought to cater for the motorist's every need – from a gallon of petrol to a new car. The garage's "service depot" was at Douglas Road. Stermat hardware store now occupies this building.

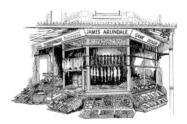
The Arundale name is a long-established and still familiar business name in Colwyn Bay. This is a 1926 advertisement for James Arundale,s fruit, fish, poultry and art florist shop at 93 Abergele Road in the Aberdeen, part of the Victoria Arcade, on the opposite corner of Erw Wen Road to the Midland Garage.

The Victoria Arcade includes all the premises from the corner of Greenfield Road as far as the corner of Erw Wen Road. The Victoria Restaurant stood on the corner during the early years of the century, but furniture dealers Aston & Son of Lyons House were one of the longest standing businesses here, from around 1910 until the 1970s. Local council minutes for 1909 report a curious accident to James Arundale's horse and cart whilst standing in front of his shop, on the corner of Erw Wen Road. It appeared the horse took fright through the alleged negligence of the water cart driver, when watering the road past the premises. The council's highways committee considered the matter but denied liability for the accident.

Painters and decorators Messrs. Jones Brothers moved into these premises at Kingston House in January 1912, having previously been at 2 Victoria Buildings (4 doors away from the new shop). The new shop was "fitted up to meet the needs of all those who require modern and up-to-date decorations". Prospective business and domestic customers were assured of best materials, good workmanship, and moderate charges.

TELEPHONE 286

JONES BROTHERS

Plumbers, Gasfitters, Electricians, House and Church Painters, Paperhangers and General Decorators

Kingston House, ABERGELE ROAD
COLWYN BAY.

◉

ALL KINDS OF REPAIRS TO PROPERTY UNDERTAKEN
BEST MATERIAL   GOOD WORKMANSHIP   MODERATE CHARGES
ESTIMATES AND ADVICE FREE

Tabernacl Welsh Baptist Chapel held its first service on October 3rd, 1888. The chapel had 41 members at the beginning. The gothic-fronted chapel had seating for 550 people and was built at a cost of £1,800. The Rev. William Hughes was the first minister and remained so until he left in 1891 to concentrate on his work with the Congo Institute. The building of the chapel was first mentioned in a local "Gymanfa Ganu" in June 1880, a decision was then taken that J. Williams and R. Jeffreys of Colwyn, W. Williams of Llanelian and J. J. Williams of Rhyl would be appointed to assist in the founding of the church in Colwyn Bay. Previously meetings had been held in the chemist shop of Owen Jones on Station Road.

In this late 19th century view Homan's "Haircutting Rooms" are on the right in the building which stood to the left of the Public Hall. Next door to Homan's was Williams' livery stables, which in turn was next door to J. R. Jones, saddler and harness-maker, who later moved to Conway Road. The house on the left was called Fraid Villa. All of the buildings here, apart from the Public Hall (now Theatr Colwyn) were demolished and replaced by a row of shops.

The present day Union Church (United Reformed and Baptist worship) on the corner of Seaview Road was built in 1885 as the Congregational Church. Before this building, an iron church stood on the site. During the summer 2002, services ceased to be held and the final service was on 25th August 2002.

Around 1910 if you stood at the bottom of Rhiw Road and looked left this is the view you would have seen. From the right of the row are the Royal Hotel and Restaurant; John Jones & Son, butchers at Grimsby House; Dyson & Wilkinson, bakers and grocers at Conway House; Roberts & Jones, ironmongers at Ivy Buildings and D. Llewelyn Jones, chemist at Ivy House.

The Royal Hotel on the corner of Seaview Road, c.1890.

A procession travelling through Colwyn Bay past the Congregational Church before the trams had been installed. Note the canopies on the shops near the Royal Hotel and Restaurant. A uniformed policeman can be seen walking at the front of the procession.

A view from 1914 of the row of shops opposite St. Paul's Church. D. Jones & Co. at The Carlton was a motor and cycle store; Ellis & Jones now ran the ironmongers at Ivy Buildings but D. Llewelyn Jones was still the chemist at Ivy House.

A late 19th century view of the shop which occupied the left side of Ivy House, Colwyn Bay's first stone-built house, at the top of Ivy Street (which took its name from the house). Built by Thomas Hughes in 1865, it was he who opened the grocer's shop in part of the building, and Methodist worship in Colwyn Bay first took place in this house's kitchen. Thomas Hughes was a founder member of Engedi Chapel and later Hermon Chapel on Brompton Avenue. Diamonds tobacconist and newsagent now occupy the shop.

Chapter 10 - Old Colwyn

Old Colwyn from the station, 1904. The station was opened in 1884, widened at the beginning of the 1900s and despite protests from residents and shopkeepers it closed in 1952.

Plough Terrace was alongside the turnpike at Colwyn. Animals were driven along here to the nearby slaughterhouse, which was at the rear of Evan Jones' butchers shop.

The Ship Inn, seen here on the left, is thought to have dated from the early 19th century; it was on an original coaching route and was a watering hole for horses.

Local historian Dilys Thomas relates in her book "Memories of Old Colwyn" how a young Princess Victoria and her mother, the Duchess of Kent, stopped at the Ship Inn in 1832 during a return journey from Plas Newydd for the horses to be watered. The visit was later commemorated with the naming of Princess Road in her honour.

A 1920s advertisement for the Ship Hotel.

The main road through Old Colwyn boasted five public houses within a quarter of a mile of each other; the Red Lion can be seen here on the right hand side, it was originally known as the Union Arms. Note the transport taking visitors to the Fairy Glen, it is just passing the top of Beach Road on the left of this picture, taken around 1905.

Seen here in a 1920s advertisement, Bernard Beer's pharmacy on Abergele Road was two doors away from the Sun Inn.

During the 1920s, Havana House, next door to the Post Office Buildings, was the business address of William Davies who ran a hairdressing saloon, newsagents, stationers, tobacconist and circulating library here.

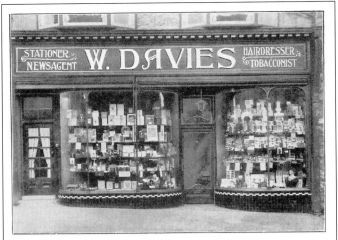

High-Class *HAIRDRESSING SALOON*

W. DAVIES

STATIONER, NEWSAGENT
TOBACCONIST, Etc.

Circulating Library

The leading Shop for Local View Post Cards, View Books, Etc.

Havana House, Old Colwyn

During the early years of the century William S. Moss was sub-postmaster of Old Colwyn Post Office, next door to Havana House, on the corner of Beach Road. The London City and Midland Bank was opposite.

A 1920s view of Abergele Road showing J. G. Wyatt's ironmonger's shop on the corner of Beach Road, next door to Havana House. It is interesting to note that the first tram appeared in Old Colwyn in 1915, they had begun to operate from Llandudno in 1907, extending to Colwyn Bay and then as far as the Queen's Hotel, Old Colwyn. The first "bus service" started up in the 1920s.

A similar view of Abergele Road to that shown on the previous page. Electricity has been installed but the tram service has yet to reach Old Colwyn, dating the photograph before 1915. On the left can be seen an often-used advertising feature of the time – a large pair of spectacle frames outside the optician's shop doorway.

The building on the left is Old Colwyn's branch of the HSBC Bank, on the corner of Cefn Road. Built in 1912 by Liverpool architects Messrs. Woolfall and Eccles, for the London City and Midland Bank Ltd. The porch of the Ship Inn can be seen on the right. A tram can be seen returning through the village having been to its furthest stop at the Queen's Hotel.

The Donkey Path was so called because a black donkey was raffled, raising £60, to enable a new path to be constructed. The original path from Min-y-Don to the beach crossed the railway line and following a fatal accident improvements were necessary to ensure the safety of all.

Records show that Beach Road was referred to as the new public carriage, horse road and public footway in around 1824. St. John's Church, built between 1899 and 1903, on the corner of Station Road and Cliff Road, can be seen in the background.

The formal opening of the Fairy Glen (previously known as "The Nant") was described as one of the outstanding events of 1904. It was given to the people of Colwyn for their enjoyment and was a picturesque wooded dingle traversed by a stream, a popular haunt of visitors.

Uwch-y-Don Poultry Farm.

Voryn Hall Holiday Camp was established in 1906 as one of the Founder Members of the National Federation of Permanent Holiday Camps, and by 1952 was, according to owners Messrs. Scarborough Holiday Chalets Ltd., one of the most successful businesses on the north Wales coast with rapidly increasing trading figures. The Hall had an entrance hall and reception; fifteen bedrooms to sleep 37 guests and 6 staff; dining room to seat 74; kitchens and a refrigeration room; three bathrooms; 32 chalets to sleep 83 guests; a recreation room with maple floor and stage; games room; balcony lounge; hard tennis court, terraced garden, children's playground; in all about 2 acres. Put up for auction on November 6th, 1952 the business was not sold as a going concern and was eventually demolished to make room for new housing.

The Queen's Hotel was built in 1889 and named in honour of Queen Victoria. The green fields seen here would eventually disappear beneath the new housing needed during the rapid expansion of Colwyn Bay and the surrounding areas. By 1915 the tram track was extended to the Queen's Hotel. When the Ministry of Food evacuated to Colwyn Bay during World War II, the Queen's Hotel was used as a staff canteen.

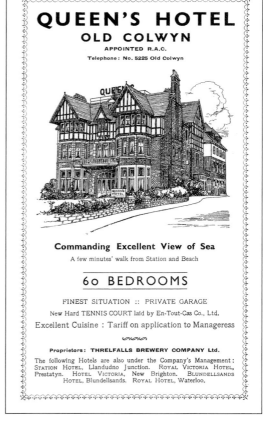

A 1931 advertisement for the Queen's Hotel which is now Queen's Court Nursing Home.

Penmaenhead Cottages, on the right, were demolished in the 1920s. Just to the top left of this picture is where The Colwyn Bay Hotel is sited.

The widening of Abergele Road at Penmaenhead in the 1930s. The reinforced concrete viaduct, built by Norwest Construction Co. Ltd, cost £16,000 and opened on June 6th, 1935. Colwyn Bay Hotel (formerly the Hotel 70 Degrees) now stands on the cliff top to the left of the picture.

An aerial view looking towards Old Colwyn from Penmaenhead before the development of the A55 Expressway.

The view from the Colwyn Bay Hotel in 1984 (then the Hotel 70 Degrees) showing the A55 Expressway which took a coastal route past Old Colwyn and Colwyn Bay.

Elizabeth Hughes and her grandson Glyn Thomas are seen outside Tunnel Cottage, Penmaenrhos. Glyn Thomas is the brother-in-law of Dilys Thomas, author of "Memories of Old Colwyn", published in 2000.

A boat trip returning to the shore at Penmaenhead. The Penmaenhead jetty can be seen in the distance.

A. & F. Wrigley's staff in Ivy Street in 1931. The little girl is Arthur Wrigley's daughter Patricia. The staff include Albert and Herbert Wright, Curly (Bertie) Barwiss and Bertie Williams.

During the 1940s and 1950s Arthur Wrigley used this van, a converted St. John's ambulance, to develop and print proofs of wedding photographs.

The A. & F. Wrigley shop was at 50 Seaview Road. Here Arthur Wrigley's daughter Patricia is seen outside the shop with a shop assistant dressed in a Kodak-Girl's striped dress.

A. & F. Wrigley's photographic workroom at Ivy Street. Frank Wrigley is on the far right.

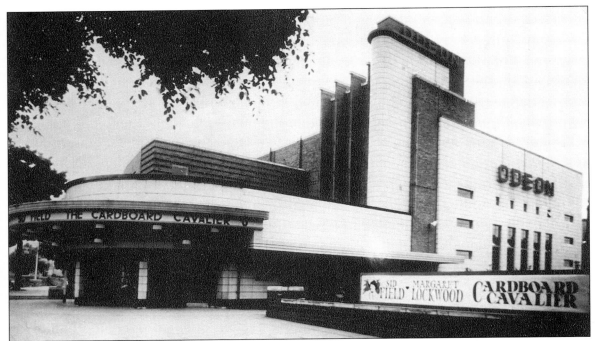

A view of the Odeon cinema taken by Wrigleys. The cinema was at the corner of Conwy Road and Marine Road, designed by architect Harry Weedon, and seated a total of 1,706. Having opened in April 1936, it was renamed the Astra Entertainment Centre in June 1967, when it also had bingo available but it finally closed in October 1986 and was demolished soon after. Swn-y-Mor retirement apartments now occupy the site.

Another photograph taken by Wrigley's shows the cast of the Baptist Church's missionary play in 1934 / 35. Among the cast were: May Anderton, Winifred Rigby (supervisor at Woolworths), Muriel Hamilton, Nora Moseley, Len Browning (manager of L.C.M. Butchers, Abergele Road), Vera (Drapers shop, West End), Albert Rigby (Arthur Wrigley's son-in-law), Eric Newell.

Mrs. Carver's 5th year class at Ysgol Bryn Elian, 1977. Left to right: seated on the floor – Nicky, Mark, Michael; seated on chairs – Carol, Hilary, Mandy, Eirian, Mrs. Carver, Janet, Eunice, Jayne; standing – Lynne, Ann, Jackie, Carol, Sian, Jacquetta, Bridget, Christine, Julie, Fiona, Romaine; back row: Dafydd, Dyfed, Clwyd, Peter, John. The new school had moved to its new buildings in 1976, Colwyn High School having been split into Eirias High and Bryn Elian Schools in September, 1974. Built on Parciau land at the top of Windsor Drive, staff and pupils previously based at Pendorlan School moved into the new Bryn Elian School.

St. John's Playgroup, 1985.

Headmistress Eluned Roberts with a group of Ysgol Bod Alaw pupils who were at the school during the early 1950s. Miss Roberts was headmistress between 1950 and 1965.

A group of pupils from Ysgol Bod Alaw on top of St. Paul's Church in 1964, with headmistress Eluned Roberts on the left and teacher Miss Shelbourne on the right.

A class at Ysgol Bod Alaw in 1965, with teacher Miss Shelbourne on the left and headmistress Eluned Roberts on the left.

Teachers Miss Shelbourne and Miss Wyn with their class in the original Ysgol Bod Alaw building on Riviere's Avenue c. 1970. Among the pupils are: Gareth Evans, Sian Humphries, Andrew Jones, Eleanor Jones, Sian Jones, Rhys Latter, Jane Lloyd, Andrew Lunn, Malcolm McBreeze, Ceri Moffat, David Pritchard, Charles Roberts, Gareth Roberts, Anna Williams and Mark Wincup.

Ysgol Bod Alaw moved in to this new school building in January 1972 and it was officially opened on November 28th of that year. The site of this new purpose-built school was Barberry Hill, which was originally home to Colwyn Bay's Technical College before it moved to the present Llandrillo College. Ysgol Bod Alaw opened on March 1st, 1950 in Bod Alaw, Riviere's Avenue – the street having been named after conductor Jules Riviere who's Colwyn Bay home had been at this house which he had named Bod Alaw.

Ysgol Bod Alaw's nativity play c. 1973. Among the cast are: Sian Humphries, Andrew Jones, Eleanor Jones, Sian Jones, Rhys Latter, Jane Lloyd, Andrew Lunn, David Pritchard, Charles Roberts, Gareth Roberts, Anna Williams and Mark Wincup.

Teacher Mr. Eynon's class at Ysgol Bod Alaw receiving their cycling proficiency certificates from an officer from North Wales Police, c. 1980. Present in the picture are, at the back, from the left, Headmaster T. Gwynn Jones (Headmaster from 1966 to 1982) and Mr. Eynon is standing next to him. The other gentleman and the Police Officer's names are not known. The pupils, from left to right, are Matthew, John Birdsall, David Parry, Dafydd Hughes, Dewi Williams, Rhys Ifor Jones, Darryl Williams, Iwan Tudur Jones, Meirion, Eifion Blease, Llyr Williams, Gareth Lamb Jones, Alwyn Richards, David Glyn Roberts, Elgan, Eleri, Sian Heulwen, Alex Booth, Jane Meredith, Enfys Jones, Helen, Iona Davies, and Gwenno Lloyd. Kneeling at the front are Gareth Roberts and Dewi Roberts.

Headmaster Dilwyn Price and pupils from Llandrillo-yn-Rhos Junior School at Colwyn Bay Library helping to celebrate the launch of Clwyd Library Service's publication "Llandrillo-yn-Rhos". The book features a short play, Ednyfed Fychan, which was performed by the pupils at the launch on June 24th, 1993. The play, written by the Rev. E. James Evans, tells the story of Ednyfed Fychan who built Llys Euryn Palace in Rhos-on-Sea in the 13th century. The ruins of the building provided the setting for the original performance of the play. The book brought together two key turn of the century texts on Llandrillo-yn-Rhos – the Rev. Venables Williams' "An Archaeological History of Llandrillo-yn-Rhos and the Immediate Neighbourhood", published about 1898 and the Rev. T. E. Timothy's "Llandrillo-yn-Rhos : A Souvenir", published in 1910.

Mochdre Primary School, 1946.

Mochdre School, 1946.

Dinner time at Mochdre Primary School, 1946.

Pendorlan Secondary Modern School on East Parade opened in 1930 and was demolished to make way for the A55 Expressway. The building was left empty in 1974 when Colwyn High School, of which it was part, was split and the staff and pupils moved to the new Ysgol Bryn Elian.

Preparations for Christmas in the Home Economics class during the 1960s at Pendorlan School.

A music group photographed by Mr. E. Emrys Jones, geography teacher at Pendorlan School, c.1973.

One of the many clog dancing groups taught by Welsh Teacher Owen Huw Roberts during his time at Pendorlan Secondary Modern, Colwyn High and Bryn Elian Schools, between 1960 and 1987.

A late 1950s or early 1960s view of a geography class at Pendorlan School, this photograph was taken by geography master Mr. E. Emrys Jones.

Above right: Seen here c. 1910, the higher grade school was built in 1903 and became the secondary school in 1920, then later the grammar school. The building is now part of Eirias School.

Right: The sixth form at Eirias High School in 1968.

Colwyn Bay Grammar School May 1962. Headmaster Mr. R. E. Roberts is accompanied by staff and pupils of the school. Mr. Roberts retired in 1974.

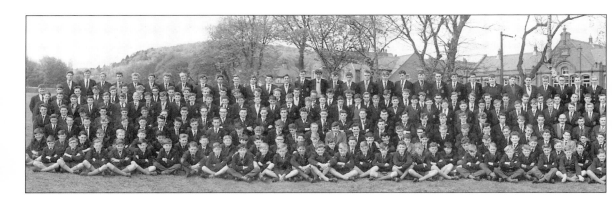

Senior staff at Eirias High School in 1975. Arthur Davy, E. Roland Jones, Pat Roberts, Jim Allen, Julie Jones, Bill Beattie.

Miss M. E. Jones, Head of Biology, with pupils from form VI at Eirias High School in 1970-71, participating in the Plant a Tree Scheme in the Coed Coch Road area of Old Colwyn.

Eirias High School's "three little maids" during rehearsal for the school's production of "The Mikado" in 1969.

Members of the cast of Eirias High School's production of the Mikado in 1969.

Founded by Mr. T. G. Osborn, M. A., Rydal Mount School opened on September 19th, 1885, taking its name from the house in which it began Rydal Mount, (pictured above), on the corner of Lansdowne Road and Pwllycrochan Avenue. The School grew steadily, buildings eventually being added along Lansdowne Road as far as Queens Drive. The Centenary History of the School records that the new Science Building (now knows as the Costain Building) planned in 1929 was conceived in the mind of Rydals architect Sidney Colwyn Foulkes (as shown in the drawing below), he envisaged its eventual completion by the addition of a worthy and adequate Hall. The Memorial Hall on Queens Drive to commemorate the 43 Old Rydalians lost during World War II opened in 1957. Rydal School bought the Pwllycrochan Hotel in 1951 to be used as a junior school, and merged with Penrhos College in 1995 becoming known as Rydal Penrhos.

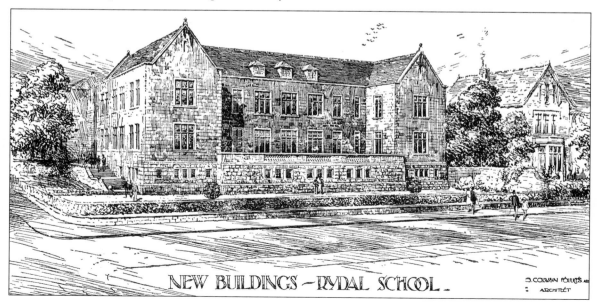

NEW BUILDINGS – RYDAL SCHOOL.

J. COLWYN FOULKES ARIBA
ARCHITECT

In 1890 the Congo Training Institute, abbreviated locally to "The Congo", was established in the new Congo House on Nant-y-Glyn Road, by the Rev. William Hughes, pastor of the Welsh Baptist Churches at Old Colwyn (Calfaria), Llanelian and later Tabernacl in Colwyn Bay. The aim of the Institute was to give African students a Christian education and a craft apprenticeship. They would then return home as self-supporting missionaries. Later renamed the African Institute it finally closed in 1911.

The Rev. William Hughes is seen here with a group of students at the Congo Institute. The Rev. Hughes is at the centre of the picture, wearing a top hat.

Who could have predicted that an advertisement placed in the local paper by Gladys Rickards (neé Wilson) in 1947 would see the forming of a drama society which is still going strong some 55 years later. That original advertisement drew 20 responses and the resulting meeting in February of that year saw the birth of Colwyn Abbey Players. The membership in those early days was 2/6 a year.

Among members in this early post-performance gathering are Joyce Dodd, Sidney Fisher, Mr. & Mrs. Fred Williams, Mr. & Mrs. Peacock, Gladys Rickards, Walter Hartill, Olive Wignall, Jim Wignall, Philip Wilson and Gwyneth Parry.

The cast of Ibsen's drama "A Doll's House" performed at the Pier Pavilion in the autumn of 1948. Gladys Rickards and Jim Wignall were among the cast.

Emlyn Williams' play "The Light of Heart" was performed at the Pier Pavilion in the spring of 1950. The cast included Joyce Dodd, Jimmy Wignall, Gladys Rickards and Bill Parry.

The Abbey Players' visit to the Pavilion in February 1951 was to perform "Pink String and Sealing Wax" by Roland Pertwee. Among the cast were Derry Rickards, Tom Rowlands, Tom Gauge, Beryl Thomas, Joan Brooksbank, Joyce Dodd and Gladys Rickards.

Gerald Savory's "George and Margaret" was the play chosen for performance in November 1953. Pictured here from left to right, back row: Derry Rickards, Clare Owen, Peter Rickards; front row: Walter Hartill, Margaret Wilkinson, Joyce Dodd and Reg Large sitting on the arm of the chair.

Among many competition successes over the years was winning first prize at the Colwyn Bay Drama Festival for Oscar Wilde's "The Importance of Being Earnest". Gladys Rickards holds the trophy accompanied by many of the members, among them Reg Large, Walter Hartill, Margaret Wilkinson, Betty Woodbridge, Christine Hartill, Olive Wignall, Derry Rickards and Peter Rickards.

Raymond Dyer's farce "Wanted - One Body" was the choice for October 1966. Peter Rickards, Peter Birkhead, Gwyneth Parry, Rosemary Brough, Janet Davies and Mary Norris can be seen in this scene from the play.

A social gathering. Back row, left to right: Owen Jones, Rosemary Brough, Dennis Carter, Mary Norris, Peter Rickards, June Gleave, Chris Swayle. Seated: Margaret Carter, Mr. & Mrs. Tom Gauge, Elsie Dodd.

In October 1971 the Prince of Wales Theatre was the venue for the Abbey Players' production of Derek Benfield's farce "Post Horn Gallop". Mmebers of the cast included Peter Rickards, Tony Williams, Paul Winkles, Geoff Williams, Gareth Owen, Mary Norris, Elsie Dodd, Beryl Holmes, June Gleave and Jack Topham.

"Jack the Ripper" performed by Merle McCulluch, Maud Jackson, Michael Norris, Marjorie White, Hilda Hall, Bryn Jones and others.

Among the cast of "The Heiress" were Nigel Cooper, Miriam Turner, Sharon Rickards, Margaret Villiers-Jones, Gladys Rickards, Keith Toy, June Gleave and Mary Norris.

Arthur Miller's drama "The Crucible" was performed in January 1986. Among the fine cast at the Prince of Wales Theatre were: Jonathan Crook, Peter Rickards, John Barclay, Sharon Rickards, Wendy Tout Hughes, Jemma Marlor, Maurice Clark, Ann Walker, Ghislaine Dell, Penny Dewhurst, Paula Stevenson, John Hughes, Sandra Phythian, Cindy Crook, Martin Taylor, Peter Bloomfield and Chris McGoran.

An early 20th century May Day procession travelling along Abergele Road in the direction of Old Colwyn, passing the bottom of Rhiw Bank Avenue.

MAY QUEENS

For many years, Colwyn Bay's outstanding event had been the May Queen Festival. Residents and visitors endeavoured to make it a bright and happy day for the children. The young lady who was honoured by being elected as May Queen for the year was nominated by the voting of the school children of the district and then the Town Council made the decision.

After a procession of the Queen, Queen Elect and their Courts in decorated carriages through the town, the Queen was crowned in the Pier Pavilion by the ruling Queen, who then handed over the sceptre of office to her successor.

The simple pageantry of the Crowning Ceremony and the subsequent proceedings were most attractive.

Thousands visited the town on "May Day" to view the procession and the delightful entertainments, which were given entirely by the children.

Queen of the May in 1912 was Iris Ashby and her ladies-in-waiting were Yvonne Lucas and Marguerite Ashby. Her coronation and subsequent celebrations were held at the Pier Pavilion. Queen Iris wore a gown of white satin and a full court train of white brocade embroidered with small bunches of pink roses.

For the procession, Queen Iris rode in a state coach in which her throne of roses was placed on a bank of moss decorated with white and mauve lilac, and a canopy of pink and white May blossom, on top of which was a crown of mauve irises. 4-horses, with 2 postillions and 4 footmen drew the carriage.

May Queen for 1928, Doris Williams was a popular choice; she was elected by the Town Council. 9-year-old Doris was a pupil at Argyle House School, Greenfield Road, daughter of Mr. & Mrs. John Stanley Williams, Grove Road, Colwyn Bay.

1928. Mr. Joe and Doris leaving the Cenotaph. Doris looked very dainty and pretty in a beautiful gown of ivory white satin, it had a Victorian bodice and the long skirt was trimmed with silver lace and may blossom, it had a 5 yard train. The Court dressmakers, Messrs. Dickens & Jones, Regent Street, London, supplied the robe.

1928. The procession of Queen Elect Doris and her Court through the town, the Queen travelled in a 4-horse coach, with coachmen resplendent in gold braid. Headed by the Old Colwyn and Llanddulas bands, the procession made its accustomed tour of the town en-route for the Pier Pavilion. It was voted the largest and most varied pageant ever seen at Colwyn Bay. Here they are seen travelling along Abergele Road towards Old Colwyn, passing the boarded up ironmonger's shop of Ellis, Hands and Dean; Tabernacl Welsh Baptist Chapel is to the right and the Rialto Picture House in the Public Hall building (now Theatr Colwyn) is to the left. Every vantage point was used to get the best views of the procession.

Among Queen Doris' entourage were her six mounted bodyguards – Jack Hadley, Arthur Webburn, P. Arundale, J. Sifleet, P. Morris, R. Thomas – two of whom can be seen here riding through the town.

The 1928 procession passes the bottom of Grove Road.

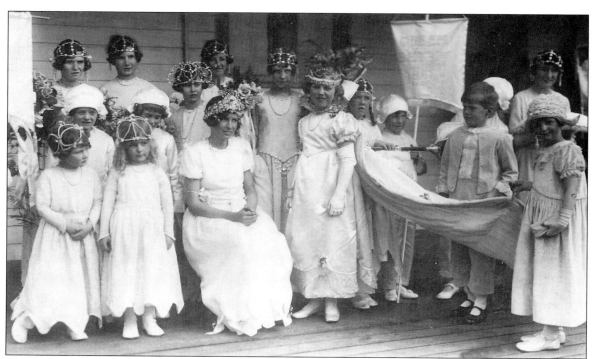

1929. Queen Doris has just crowned Queen Betty as May Queen.

The Mochdre Rose Queen Festival, 1948.
Queen Barbara Jones and her escort arrive for
the crowning ceremony.

The Tan Lan May Queen Festival, 1949. May Queen Elvira is crowned by the British Railway Queen, Beryl Parker, of Hull, at the recreaction ground in Tan Lan, Old Colwyn.

1948 Tan Lan May Queen Brenda Jones being crowned by Miss Robinson of The Croft, Colwyn Bay.

1981 carnival day at Colwyn Bay – one of the many Morris Dancing troupes dance past the Union Church as the procession travels through the town along Abergele Road to Eirias Park for the day's activities.

Despite being a rain-soaked event Rhos-on-Sea's 1981 Carnival was well attended and much enjoyed. Colwyn's Mayor Dr. Janet Williams opened the proceedings and crowned the Queen and Gary Wilmot undertook the duties of compere for the afternoon.

Archdruid Dyfed leads the Proclamation Ceremony in preparation for the Royal National Eisteddfod of Wales' visit to Colwyn Bay in 1910, at the Gorsedd Circle built at the Flagstaff Estate (now home to the Welsh Mountain Zoo), by permission of owner Walter Whitehead.

A half-day holiday was requested of and granted by the local council, Colwyn Bay & Colwyn Urban District Council, on September 7th, 1909 for the Proclamation Ceremony. It was also suggested that "as liberal a display of bunting as possible be made" in the town, and that the members of the council join the procession to the Flagstaff for the ceremony.

The commemorative postcard issued by the Daily News for the 1910 Eisteddfod.

The 1910 Eisteddfod Pavilion seen here in the process of being erected by Messrs. L. H. Woodhouse & Co. of Nottingham, to the design of Messrs. Darbyshire and Smith of Manchester, on the playing fields of Dinglewood School, Greenfield Road. The Pavilion was expected to accommodate 10,000 people.

The interior of the 1910 Pavilion ready for the Eisteddfod which ran from September 13th to the 17th.

The first Gorsedd ceremony took place on Tuesday with the procession of Bards leaving the town hall on Conwy Road at 8.15a.m. The procession should have proceeded to the Flagstaff but because of the distance involved the welcome ceremony took place at Rydal Fields.

From the Town Hall the
procession proceeded to Rydal
Fields; following the ceremony
there the procession continued to
the Pavilion.

Archdruid Dyfed leads the
Gorsedd Ceremony, welcoming
the Royal National Eisteddfod
to Colwyn Bay.

A representative group of Eisteddfodwyr taken in the grounds of Coed Derw on September 13th, 1910. From left to right they are, standing: Sir E. Vincent Evans, Sir J. Prichard Jones, Mr. T. J. Williams, Mr. J. Morris, Sir Marchant Williams; and sitting: Miss Hartley, Miss Amy Preece, Sir J. Herbert Roberts, M.P., Mrs. T. J. Williams and Mrs. Mary Davies.

The honourable secretaries of the various committees of the 1910 Eisteddfod. From left to right they are, standing: J. O. Davies, Literary Committee; Llewelyn Davies, Music Committee; H. R. Parry (Bwlchydd Mon), Gorsedd Committee; and sitting: William Jones, C.E., Arts and Science Committee; T. R. Roberts (Asaph), General Secretary; H. V. Doughty Davies, General Purposes Committee; Joseph H. Roberts, Finance Committee.

The 1910 Eisteddfod Crown was designed and presented by Messrs. W. Jones & Sons, Jewellers, of Station Road. The successful bard at Wednesday's ceremony was the Rev. W. Crwys Williams of Brynmawr, Monmouthshire, for his poem "Ednyfed Fychan", a famous Welshman who had historic connections with Llandrillo-yn-Rhos.

The Bardic Chair for 1910 was designed by Messrs. Porter & Elcock, and made and presented by D.Allen & Sons of Station Road. The successful bard at Thursday's ceremony was R. Williams Parry for his poem "Yr Haf" – "The Summer".

EISTEDDFOD GENEDLAETHOL FRENHINOL CYMRU

"Y Gwir yn Erbyn y Byd"

"Duw a Phob Daioni"   "Iesu, Na'd Gamwaith"

"Dan Nawdd Duw a'i Dangnef"

AWST 4, 5, 6, 7, 8, 9, 1947

BAE COLWYN

(YN Y PAFILIWN, PARC EIRIAS, BAE COLWYN)

The Royal National Eisteddfod of Wales visited Colwyn Bay once again in August 1947 – this was the first post-war Eisteddfod to be held in North Wales.

For the 1947 Eisteddfod the Gorsedd Circle had been built at Eirias Park, where Archdruid Wil Ifan led the Gorsedd Ceremony.

Archdruid Wil Ifan led the Eisteddfod ceremonies when Rev. Griffith John Roberts (Benellt), rector of Nantglyn, won the crown on Tuesday for his composition "Glyn y Groes" – "Valle Crucis" and J. Tudor Jones (Euddog), a native of Llaneilian Anglesey, won the chair on Thursday for his composition "Maelgwn Gwynedd".

For the 1947 Eisteddfod the spacious pavilion was built in a beautiful setting in Eirias Park, The contractors were Messrs. L.H. Woodhouse & Co. of Nottingham who were also responsible for the 1910 pavilion.